ACKNOWLEGEMENT

INSPIRATION — Today's OLIGARCHY, more powerful than Kings, Dictators and all of history's tyrants, is firmly controlling our destiny. This time is our last chance to wrest control of our own future.

LEARNED COLLABORATORS — Friends and family have been helpful in this effort, some because they knew I'd annoy them until they said, "Oh I agree with everything you said here, and a few who took time to add thoughtful comments, all of which are appreciated.

Son Trout-Bood-C4 had relevant insights as well as Undercover Bob. Another Nameless Undercover sent me some fine Scotch, which I should've sent him for his professional efforts here too. I'll have to hand deliver some so we can celebrate it together.

CONGRESS — The most lackluster bunch in my memory. If they'd have done their job, they wouldn't have to read and adopt all my recommendations, which follow.

Forward

"The Best Way To Predict
The Future Is To Invent It."[1]

Without reasonable, measurable goals and flexible plans to achieve those goals, failure is the usual consequence.

This outcome has been proven time and again, by the lack of individual achievement — by volunteer organizations squabbling incessantly rather than achieving — by Corporations ordering you to "Press One For English" which you still can't understand — and by whole nations, with today's America as a prime example.

Nothing worthwhile is accomplished. We just react to immediate needs and the crises of the moment — usually due to **no Goals and no Long Range Flexible Plans**.

America has just raised the Debt Limit to $20,000,000,000,000 (20 trillion) dollars, an intolerable national debt. Is there an achievable plan to pay it off? If not, then we should take the President and the whole damned Congress outback and hang 'em all!

Our recent health care, wasted five years, amply demonstrates a clever and well thought out plan on how to force everybody further under the Government's thumb. The "Everybody has a Doctor" notion is a good thing to all Americans, but what was approved was too lopsided, full of lies and unintended consequences **(so they say?)**.

Just as important is the fact that Pelosi and Reid schmoozed it through Congress using smoke and mirrors and then capped it all off by telling your Congressional Misrepresentative that "……….. you'll have to pass it before you can read it" — bet most of them still don't understand it, even if they did get to read it!

Some Americans are finally paying attention it seems and they don't like how they're being screwed. A comprehensive and all encompassing plan might have come to a national consensus.

Helping to insure everyone is a lofty idea, and I agree with the thought, but it gets an "**F**" in Long Range Planning School, a DC test-bed for the "New Math" I'm positive!

The Socialists are organizing our destiny by desperately trying to keep the poor enslaved in welfare where their votes are easily controlled.

The middle class is continually squeezed by inflation, Gruberized taxation, unimaginable political correctness and government regulation.

The top end's fat cats don't care one whit about our plight, only the rapidly expanding World Oligarchy they are part of.

"Hussain...

You know, If you contribute to the family's Foundation, I'm sure we can find a few dozen retired F16's for your air force. And by the way, we're having a bar-be-que Saturday! Why don't you and Daxia come on over — about three?"

Best Regards — Hill & Bill[2]

A PLAN

Are there <u>any</u> America goals?
Any plans to create some?
Any answers to those Questions?

"No" and "No" and "No" I bet!

Broad AMERICAN goals should be emblazoned on buildings, our money, our souls — and taught from pulpits and in classrooms. Specific, interim goals are more difficult to define but they're as necessary as leaves are to a tree.

It is clear that America is sinking, and that seems largely due to partisan bickering, diminished States Rights, uncontrolled special interest lobbying in every effort and to elected officials not representing their constituents now and in the recent past, but meekly following orders from leaders who have no balls.

Let's do away with those positions and just put all the proposed laws in a big hat and have the janitor pick one. That'd be the new law.

A more relevant and scary question is, "Are we ignorant of some fat-cat, Socialized master plan? Are we being **Progressively Sorosed**? Is our hard won National identity being **UN**'d and **OPEK**'ed and **Politically Overcorrected**?"

The "Low Information" voter accepts what is going on around him, blindly complying, and obeying. Don't they question anything?

"Why is the Keystone Pipe not finished?"

"Why is inflation up 38% in 15 years?"

"Why are kids dropping out of high school?"

"Why is gun violence rising?"

"Where are all the <u>good</u> jobs?"

"Why are there so many illegal aliens?"

"Why don't people get married anymore?"

"Why are we always at war in the Middle East?"

"Why do Muslims want to kill us?"

"Why aren't Archie Bunker reruns on TV?"

"Why are some street signs not in English?"

"Why are people getting so fat?"

Has our over-connected world obliterated our "Made in USA" image? Have we ineffectively meddled in too many neighborly affairs to the point where our might has turned to MUSH?

Today's Middle East is a prime example of haywire hegemony by the ISIL, by Vladimir Putin and all due to **our incomprehensible foreign policy.**

Don't Forget History..........

In the late 1930s Hitler was taking over most of Europe and taking aim at the United Kingdom, while at the same time, Italy's Benito Mussolini was consolidating his hold on and around the Mediterranean.

Before Adolph had begun his European realignment, the Imperial Japanese had been steadily trying to absorb their edge of the Pacific. That's when the legendary Chinese Flying Tigers were forming under the tutelage of Claire Chennault. Perhaps Japan was persuaded to attack Pearl Harbor as a warning?

Had Hitler stayed on the French side of the English Channel — had Mussolini not ventured into North Africa and if Hirohito stayed away from Hawaii, they all might have successfully managed their conquests. But, they wanted it all and decided to shoot V2s at the UK, and then, after Pearl Harbor was attacked, the US was also firmly into it all, with the rest of the world.

The strategic mistake made by those three dictators was in not being satisfied with their conquests to date — they got together and decided they wanted the American Continent as well. That was a short summary of the geopolitical politics from 1935 to 1945.

75 Years Later

Today's world is starting to resemble the 1940s, and maps are being redrawn. The Middle East quagmire is central in today's history lesson, with its tribes gerrymandering hunks of the oil empires all the while chopping each other up over ancient fundamental promises of free virgins.

Eastern Europe is again the target, this time of the Empire rebuilding Russian strongman Vladimir Putin. He's been saber rattling all over the Ukrainian countryside — some opined he's solidifying a new pathway to the Black Sea where the Russian fleet is preeminent.

I believe Putin doesn't want the Ukraine to join and thereby strengthen NATO. Since the current American administration has more or less told NATO, "You're on your own" when Obama pulled out of George Bush's promise to put a modern missile defense system in Poland as a deterrent to future Russian hegemony.

Where's another Reagan when you need him? NATO allies are not strong enough to challenge Putin on their own and therefore Eastern Europe is anticipating another Cold War with it as the prize.

The ISIS bunch is trying to redesign Middle East borders while Sunni Muslims, who've been mad at Shia Muslims for centuries are mixing it up with the Kurds — Iran is pissed at the Saudi's and all the while radicalized ISIS Muslims are venturing around the world, randomly shooting up the countryside just to keep everybody else on edge.

What about China and their full speed ahead efforts to expand and modernize their war machine with their copies of US battlewear? They are building new Chinese islands to control seaways that they felt are too close to their mainland and are constantly cyber hacking everybody else. The whole world is again on the brink of Armageddon.

Is the US in the same position as it was in 1939? Not quite. Not yet. So maybe this is the final opportunity for America to regroup and to reconstitute itself while the rest of the world is hyperventilating. Our current level of support is encouraging others to support themselves.

Once achieved, the goals outlined further on will put America at the head table again.

We've Lost Control!

We've decisively won wars and rehabilitated the vanquished where there was just cause, **a goal and a plan.** We've been mortified in Korea and Vietnam, and continually In the Middle East by centuries-old Muslim Jihads.

Are you aware that the US Navy was first created by the Continental Congress about 1794 to fight the Barbary Pirates (Muslims) along the North Africa coast? They were holding every seafaring nation hostage, demanding ransom for return of their crewmen, ships and cargo.

The US Marines on our 19th century sailing ships had leather collars on their uniforms to protect their necks against the Muslim Pirates' penchant for trying to separate them from their heads — waaaaay back then! That's how our Marines got the name "Leather Necks" and their anthem referring, "to the ♪ shores of ♪ Trip-O-li ♪ " — that's Tripoli, Libya — remember Qaddafi? The US Navy fought two wars there in the early 19th Century against Muslims.

The bad-guy Barbary Pirates in that same part of the world now, are called ISIS, Boko-Haram, Somali Pirates, etc.. Watch a true update of their current efforts. See the movie "Captain Phillips".

The Muslim religion has been existing peacefully, or at least out of sight in the US for many years. But, its fundamental Sharia cancer and its terrorists are also immigrating here now, and beginning to infect us just like they have in the UK, France, Spain the Philippines, Indonesia, Australia and most any place their disease is allowed to fester **unchecked**! They're a boil on our collective ass! Remember that 14 of them graduated American flight schools just before 9/11/01.

Our education system is trying to rewrite history to shield students from understanding how we've evolved as a nation, while the internet smothers them with hedonistic pursuits and the hidden recruiting of aberrant fundamental societies.

There is no Just **Goal** in place yet, to vanquish these enemies again or any semblance of a plan to achieve that outcome. Modern warfare there might dictate carpet-bombing the Middle East as a last resort — but if we don't soon set American Foreign Policy goals and get control of our hegemony, it might be the **only resort there.**

With a lofty goal, a good plan and determination, we went to the moon — yet our kids can't make change today, or pinpoint Hawaii on a globe without Goggling it. College kids in Texas couldn't even tell what Country was in the Civil War or who won? Some of them didn't know who the Vice President is???

No Child Left Behind was also a good and lofty goal, but the plan to get them on the bus also needs a kick in its behind.

They are quitting cursive writing classes! Maybe they intend to teach smoke signals — how will they ever write a resume? **OMG, I forgot** — they have instant, global, Googlized, Facebooked and Twittered thought transference! Just wiggle your fingers a little. No punctuation, no caps, no nuance — nothing, just **"Text LOL LOL".**

We've run short and paid exorbitant fuel prices, yet we have our own massive untapped natural resources. Surely we can devise a plan to satisfy diverse goals such as protecting the environment and at the same time exploiting natural resources.

Both goals are for the common good. Any other worthwhile goal for that matter can be achieved, but only with good,

FLEXIBLE PLANS!

My first milestone is to define these overall goals as they pertain to America and Americans **ONLY**. No consideration must be given <u>at this point</u> to "if", or "how", or "how much" — **only "what" <u>we</u> want to achieve**.

Once that list is complete and carved in stone, and printed on our money, then the plans to get there and to pay for it all must be created.

Goals must also be part of the 2016 Presidential Platform. I'll start this exercise by listing goals I'd like America to embrace — **plus my 2¢ on why and how**. I'm sure you can add or subtract or modify my list, but discussion has to start somewhere and might pique the interest of some of our enlightened legislators — even this new herd of wannabe Presidents.

While this may seem at first like a rant against politicians and bureaucrats, I am really only speaking out against how American **apathy** has allowed our government to devolve. After all, bureaucrats are voters too — and there's plenty of them! Washington DC and its surrounding posh Virginia and Maryland suburbs are a "**Sanctuary City**" where Politicians, Bureaucrats and Lobbyist can get away with anything, just like border crashers can in San Francisco! There's no recourse for screwing everybody else just to benefit yourself or your handlers!

Politics

November, 1956 was my first presidential vote — Dwight Eisenhower. I voted for him in his second term campaign, against Adlai Stevenson and when he had Richard Nixon as his VP. I wasn't involved in anything political in those days, but I seemed to always believe that business was the engine that drove the world.

Heroes then were Eisenhower and Patton — or business magnates like Henry Ford and Rockefeller — visionaries like Edison and Einstein, achievers like the Wright brothers, Glen and Armstrong.

Today's heroes are overpaid sports figures, bare-midriff'd tarts or loud, over-privileged Hollywood kids licking donuts. Don't get me wrong. I don't have anything against them personally — but, what do they represent?

Today's culture has become a vast hedonistic, reality TV'd, texted and Facebooked wasteland where achievement is only celebrated if it's got big bucks or big boobs attached. Meanwhile the US is on a rapid downhill decline into politically corrected mediocrity and socialism.

I tried, back in the 70s and 80s, to do my part by becoming a Republican Committeeman — a lackey in big city machine-politics. It was always fun and always hard work getting the vote out. Being a Republican in Philadelphia was usually frustrating because we most always lost and when we did win, the jerk became a despised power broker who engineered back-room deals only representing his State Politician buddies — not me. Everybody was a fireman, a cop or a crossing guard — all Democrats (by decree).

I didn't vote for Obama because his politics — his Hollywood and Chicago cronies, are way too far left for me. I might have if he was more centrist, because he had leadership qualities seldom exhibited by career politicians — or so I thought at the time.

It seems clear now that he is and was driven then by forces most of us were very naive about. He seems to be a pawn of world power-brokers, exemplified by the likes of the "Soros's" of the world. They direct world government with Obama-like puppets engineering our destiny. We were too dumb to understand that then, even if we were paying attention.

If we are now, not so dumb and paying attention too, do we have the passion our forefathers did? Unfortunately, I don't believe we have any balls anymore — black Americans seem more empowered to fight for what they believe than white Americans do??

Obama today (9/4/2015), seems to have gone back on all his campaign rhetoric, but keeping true to redistributing my wealth and welcoming **all** comers to US largess. The July 4th 2009 Pocono (Pennsylvania), Record (a newspaper — remember them?) had a front-page article analyzing why voter turnout continually declines and the author correctly surmised the reason is that the contemporary American voter doesn't give a damn anymore. Their votes didn't seem to mean anything. The outcome of the 2010 Congressional makeover, while promising, might just as well have never occurred for all the good it did.

Everyone I talk to, no matter their professed political affiliation, all express the same withdrawal from a malfunctioning system — and from State and Federal legislators who do not work for you and I, but only to protect their political tenure.

Obama is the perfect commercial for learning how to speak in public. I firmly believe every student should have "required" public speaking class. Caroline Kennedy lost out in her bid to continue in the Kennedy dynasty as a US Senator a few years ago, purely because she spoke publically like pants-dragging teenagers do, with tattoos on their asses and rings in their royal bellybuttons. The fact that she was unqualified to fill a US Senate seat didn't seem to matter to most of the political dimwits in this country.

All of Congress has high paying positions, with lavish expense accounts, better health and retirement plans than most of their constituents; so why is it so hard to see their main motive is to keep milking their golden cow — us?

Partisan bickering at every level of our Government, produces nothing of real value — no simple tax reform, just more pork barrel projects that would never pass a vote on their own merits. They used to be attached to every piece of major legislation; an ongoing litany of smoke and mirrors, with one sure result — reelection of self-serving politicians. "You'll have to pass the bill to see what's in it," — unrelated pork, attached because the bill is going to be pushed through no matter what's stuck to it.

A perfect example of the Political "Smoke and Mirrors" that goes on in Washington was the 10/20/15 maneuvering in the Senate to **not pass** the "Kate's Law" bill.[3]

Legions of pissed-off Americans became Tea Party members and were successful in backing many new legislators in recent elections.

The presence of these new members of Congress seems to have been able to block some new legislative mismanagement in the meantime, but they weren't well enough organized to make any real difference in the ACA (Obama care) debacle. Since the 2010 elections, Congress had been gridlocked. It seems to be still gridlocked, even after the resounding Congressional 2012 makeover. Nothing seems to be getting done — ever!

This gridlock has been engendered by no compromise from the left and not much more from the right. The Tea Party movement wasn't strong enough to negate the GOP's absorption and that is one of the key points that must be addressed if they ever hope to evolve on their own in the future. They were bullied into following Republican mandates — somewhat.

Imagine how effective they could be if they were the sought after legislative vote — by both of the other parties. They must remain attached to the Republican label however, until they build their numbers and influence enough to maybe present a viable Independent Presidential candidate, by 2020.

We have a president now who seems elitist and arrogant and lately on both sides of every issue, trying desperately to say anything to schmooze his uninformed Democratic leaning lemmings.

We have a President who seems to be a lousy planner and worse, seems unable to eat humble pie, and admit mistakes and revise whatever dopey plan he might have had. Thank God term-limits are imposed on that office. Even if another jackass schmoozes his way in, he's sure to be out in eight — **but by then it'll be too late!**

Political candidates who have the largest war chest usually win, regardless of qualifications. A smart business usually doesn't select a new president or CEO who didn't have management experience overseeing a similar business model. America has been selecting its Chief Executives from Congressional and Gubernatorial ranks with little thought about the necessary credentials to manage it all. All they needed was lots of cash from "Superfunds". Why not **define the preferred line of progression**, where candidates for the Presidency are nominated, **only from their ranks**?

If you were a Human Resources person creating a list of credentials necessary for a prospective high-level Corporate position, you'd probably detail expected past experiences relative to the job being applied for.

Not all the current crop of POTUS candidates will score high using these parameters, but they reflect qualities and experiences that are a **<u>starting point of life achievements that must be consdidered</u>** — that every Presidential Candidate should have.

But that isn't all by a long shot. There's also the necessary qualities of determination, leadership, and some other personal traits that are not easily quantifiable with this kind of a guideline.

Some of today's herd of establishment candidates are being rejected by polled voters in favor of some new faces on the political scene. The voting public doesn't seem to care about qualifications — only somebody who's not a **flaming POLITICIAN**!

Here is my list of past work experiences and qualifications, a starting point for US President if I was the recruiter for this job. <u>**All prospects**</u> must have been successful in most of these endeavors.

These credentials are in priority order:

Former Governor — 25% + 5% successive terms

Former US Vice President — 30%

Former Congressman — House 10% or Senate, 15%, +5% if both, with relative past Federal experience in Defense, Intelligence & Foreign Affairs + 5% ea.

Former Cabinet Head — 10%

Former military — 5%, Field Grade +5%, Combat +5%

Business owner — 5%, major + 5%, Corp. CEO + 5%

The problem seems to be money. I'm sure there are qualified candidates who may fit my basic qualifications, but are not as well connected as Hillary, Donald and Jeb are. Clinton, Trump and Bush all have immense war chests. Should that be what gets them the job? I hope not. It's too late for this election, but something has to be done — some reform to eliminate buying **any** elective office for future elections.

These percentages listed above are just <u>**one**</u> of the measurements any recruiter would have to consider. With the thought that your wisdom quotient goes up with age, I'd +/- ½ % for every year +/- 50 years old.

If those metrics were the <u>**only consideration**</u>, John Kasich would lead the list by a long shot. Buy how about a **subjective score too** — an analysis of a candidates balls, "not afraid to tell it like it is" so to speak, but always with Statesman-like decorum, a most important presidential attribute — 20%?

So far, today (1/1/16) ????
- Trump — Balls 20%, Statesman 0%
- Carson — Balls 5%, Statesman 5%
- Fiorina — Chin 10%, Stateswoman 5%
- Kristie — Balls 15%, Statesman 10%
- Paul — Balls 10%, Statesman 5%
- Kasich — Balls 10%, Statesman 10 %
- Kruse — Balls 15%, Statesman 10%
- Rubio — Balls 15%, Statesman 10%

In Trump's case, he loses a few points pretending. Some candidates seem to pretend a little in one way or another, when what I'm looking for is the feeling that I am listening to someone who is conveying a genuine, no baloney sentiment.

Trump's got to ditch the hair dye and comb-over! He obviously has wispy, white hair, and I'm sure he's earned it — but who is he trying to fool? It's a distracting character flaw in my mind (-5%). Women can get away with a bleach or dye job, but not men. I might be wrong, but I believe Margaret Thatcher had white hair and Hillary Clinton has blond — probably gray by now also, and earned as well.

The job Trump's vying for needs a real person. Show-business has rubbed off on Trump, but it won't serve him well in this arena. He's like Archie Bunker in a suit. He seems to get your attention with bluster, wise cracks and volume — not convincing, but annoying with his **"me, me, me"** prattle. I think a statesman commands respect — doesn't demand it!

Unwittingly, "People choose shiny objects all the time."[4] The glint and glitter obscures defects that the non-thinking, easily led voter misses, ignores or can't fathom. I believe at this time that Carson is the more genuine outsider and the polls were seeming to verify that, <u>early on</u>.

Trump's money and Hollywood glitter seem to be winning him his Oscar — but this isn't Hollywood, it's the whole America, the whole world stage. To his credit his showmanship may be concealing a pragmatic nature, that belies his seeming lack of control. Maybe he is the "Patton or Teddy Roosevelt or FDR, "Try something — If that doesn't work, try something else," pragmatist we need right now????

God bless him, Bernie Sanders seems a more genuine person, but warped by his Socialist agenda. He wants to give all aspirants free college. Why not require colleges to offer free tuition instead? Bet that won't work either.

I had a conversation the other day at a birthday party with an acquaintance who I thought was well informed. He questioned why I was not sure about Trump. Analyzing later why he was so enthusiastic for The Donald, the continuing conversation led me to the conclusion that, although my friend was apparently a capable rancher/farmer, businessman, he was not well informed politically — not a political junkie like me. His only qualifier was, "He's an Outsider, not one of the crooks in DC now". Trump is either politically smarter and savvy than I think (I hope) or we're in deep doo doo.

This whole crop of Presidential Candidates is generally amazing. So many have gotten into the race, it's difficult to pick the best one. I believe any of them, including Trump, and even me, could do a better job than the current administration. One or two of them will rise to the top — we hope.

Here's an interesting thought

that most haven't had I bet!

Given the immense talent and cohesive thought the whole bunch has, how do we utilize **all of them** for the greater good of America?

We currently have 16+ Republican candidates for the 2016 Presidential election. Assuming one of them is elected to fill that seat, and another as the Vice President, that leaves 14 top Republican leaders who **should** be drafted by the winner to fill Department and Agency head positions. **Wouldn't that make one hell of a leadership cadre?**

The next Republican leader of America must not let them get away. We need all of them now! Appoint each as Heads of the different Cabinets and Departments.

For instance:

- **Supreme Court** — Ted Cruz
- **Attorney General** — Chris Christy?
- **Surgeon General + HHS + VA + CDC** — Ben Carson

- **Labor Department** — Scott Walker
- **Commerce, Energy & Interior** — Carly Fiorina
- **WPA Department (new – as in the 30's)** — Mike Huckabee
- **FEMA** — Bobby Jindal
- **State Department** — Kasich or Trump or Romney
- **Defense** — John McCain
- **CIA, NSA, FBI, Homeland Security** — Giuliani
- **Treasury and Head of Federal Reserve Bank** — <u>Ron</u> Paul with orders to get back on the Gold Standard and close out the Federal Reserve.
- **Immigration & Border Security** — Perry or Rubio — Seal borders and go back to 1965 immigration quotas and procedures.
- **Education Department** — Eliminate! Return to State, local and Church control.
- **Government Restructure** — <u>Rand</u> Paul with his Libertarian view.

Maybe the GOP could convince Trump to run for one term with Kasich as VP who would fill in for the next two terms!

I'm done venting. Here's what I want you to think about. In the following pages, I've listed **b r o a d** goals — **my goals**, and I'll expand on each and suggest how I'd approach accomplishing them. There's no malice intended here. There is concern though, that we are being **manipulated — not led**.

All I'm trying to do is propose a way to make political manipulation a useless endeavor and to help some, as yet, unknown and untested leaders emerge from the oppression of an apparent creeping and global Oligarchy, one with a Socialist agenda too.

Please read on. It's not very long.

GOALS

Dollar $overeignty

Streamlined Government

Everybody Works

Complete Independence

Military & Space Superiority

Birth to Death Entitlements

Defined & Controlled Immigration

Inviolate Traditions

DOLLAR $OVEREIGNTY

What Do I Mean By That?

Why should we worry about that and why is it first on this list? Well, most of the world's economies have been trading in the US dollar because of its stability — in the past.

"The dollar's role as the world's primary reserve currency helps all of us Americans by keeping interest rates low. Foreign countries buy United States Treasury debt not just as an investment, but dollar-denominated assets are the best way to hold foreign exchange reserves." [5]

When we buy foreign commodities, which are traded in US Dollars, we set the interest rates, while those same commodities might cost more if traded in some other currency. Our "Standard and Poors" rating was downgraded a few years ago, which makes other countries wonder if the Dollar's interest will remain stable and therefore maybe they'll trade in something else, like the Euro for instance. Commodities traded with Euros may well cost us more.

The Dollar may be downgraded again if we don't get our borrowing under control. It's like your personal credit score — fill up a couple of credit cards and watch it go down. Same thing happens in the world market.

Not only do we have an almost **unimaginable annual national debt load**, but we have a Federal regime that seems incapable or maybe unwilling to get it under control. The Government's CBO has estimated through 2018, that the budget deficit will remain around **$500 to $600 billion a year**, or about 2½ percent of the gross domestic product (GDP) of the United States. After 2018, however, the budget deficit will rise past three percent of GDP, and then hit four percent by 2025".[6] **That's just the interest on our credit card!**

That's almost enough to run the Department of Defense or the VA for a whole yeeeeear! What if the Federal Reserve raises the prime rate a few points to keep inflation manageable? How much will the annual debt be then?

Could we wind up like Greece with ATMs stuck on $60 withdrawals? Our Protectorate, Puerto Rico has just declared bankruptcy. Detroit's already had to belly up. Stockton, CA, Philadelphia, Los Angeles, Harrisburg, PA, San Jose, Calif., Suffolk County, NY, Camden, NJ, Cincinnati, San Diego, San Francisco — **all on the edge**!

The SEIU (Service Employees International Union)[7] has a stronghold on most cities, which, coupled with elected City Fathers who couldn't run a car wash, much less a city, seem to be crashing this country internally while the DC crowd is doing us in globally.

Is there a Socialist undercurrent? You bet! They keep adding expensive social programs that require money we don't have. They don't cut back on other programs and pork, deemed not as important as whatever the latest new idea is — they bury the new taxes that everyone knows won't pass without hiding them in legislation using smoke and mirrors. They Gruberize **(hide the bad stuff)** in every new program.

Only in January 2015, did these new tax increases pop up, hidden in Obamacare.

Top Medicare tax went up from 1.45% to 2.35%

Top Income tax bracket is up from 35% to 39.6%
Top payroll tax went up from 37.4% to 52.2%
Capital Gains tax went up from 15% to 28%
Dividends tax went up from 15% to 39.6%
Estate tax went up from <u>nothing</u> to 55%

These taxes were all passed, obscured and Gruberized, in the Affordable Care Act of March, 2010 — a.k.a. "Obamacare", or otherwise known as **"Redistributing Your Wealth"**. It's a classic Socialist-Communist-Fascist move. Read and understand history.

To stabilize the dollar, America has to <u>eliminate</u> its monstrous foreign debt and build large reserves (**Rainy Day Funds**) for contingencies such as natural disasters and war. We have to **not borrow** Chinese and Japanese money to continue bankrolling every Progressive hand Barack Gruber Obama and his New World oligarchy has in our pocket. Maybe it's time to get back on the Gold Standard to help cement the dollar's **AAAAAAA+** rating in world financial markets.

We should set a goal to **<u>completely eliminate</u>** our deficit by a certain date and to build reserves to negate future borrowing. Why don't we set that goal at ten years? It will mean a difficult belt tightening, and maybe even a dedicated **"National Ten Year Deficit – Rainy Day Contingencies Tax"** — and determined legislators **not afraid** to build the Master Plan that'll get us there, as **priority number one**.

This first goal must be augmented by all the other goals and plans. **Social planning, Environment and other "Nice to Have" programs** must take a back seat to this one issue — it's that important. Funding for all the other goals can only increase as this most important goal is achieved...........................

STREAMLINE GOVERNMENT

This goal could easily fill volumes, especially if it were made a Government project, such as the ACA's initial release debacle. Before this gets out of hand, let me add a few personal experiences to illustrate **simple and obvious** ills.

I had uprooted myself in 2006, sold my home and became an RV vagabond for the next four years. Me and my RV were planted in a huge PA State Park (Hickory Run) as its "Campground Host" for most of 2009, when the Commerce Department advertised for "Census Taker" help. I applied and became one of the "Enumerators" who trekked throughout the Pocono Mountains along the east-central Pennsylvania border for three months in the fall of 2009. I was charged with gathering "GPS Map Spot" data which was in preparation for the actual census starting April 1, 2010.

The Department of Commerce conducts the Decennial Census of the whole US population, mainly to reapportion Congressional Districts in the US House of Representatives for each US State and Territory. Every ten years a census taker would knock on your door and ask probing questions about your household, and leave a mail-in form if you were out. They work year-round with numerous other government issues to research, but the "every ten years" effort is the one most Americans are aware of.

The actual 2010 Census included a preliminary visit by Census Enumerators, (me) who would use a hand-held GPS recorder so that each property could receive the dreaded "GPS

Map Spot". This was based on addresses of preexisting homes. "Spots" had to be added for them and for all new construction since the last decennial census.

We had directions to map every habitable spot — look under every bridge, in every cardboard box to see if some hapless citizen resided there, and if it looked lived in, the box would get **"The Spot".** Jokes opined that the Government then knew exactly where a drone could aim its missile when you didn't pay your taxes or when they wanted to send Homeland Security's troops to snatch your gun, or even if you watched too much FOX News.

<u>Meanwhile,</u> dragging a travel trailer everywhere and staying overnight here and there in campgrounds was prohibitively expensive for me, so I pursued volunteering for the US Interior Department's National Wildlife Refuge system (NWR), scattered all over the US.

This volunteer service usually provides a free RV parking spot, water, sewer and electric hookups in exchange for 20 to 30 hours per week of free labor for your 90 day commitment somewhere. It's a great deal and I got to see a lot of places and do things most people never get a chance to do. The Government gets your expertise or labor, free for 90 days at a time, here and there — **Key Deer NWR** (National Wildlife Refuge) in Florida, **Back Bay NWR** in Virginia Beach, **Erie NWR**, etc..

Working for the Government always means you need a security clearance however, even if all your doing is mowing grass. I was feeling more like James Bond every day, when my friends would say, "What did you do? the Secret Service was asking about you?" I'd say, "I'm gonna' mow gov'mint grass."

Incident #1

I was successful in negotiating a 90 day volunteer position, March, April & May 2010 with the US Interior Department at their Key Deer National Wildlife Refuge in the Florida Keys. It occurred to me that I could also do the actual 2010 Census while there, since I was already trained and had my James Bond license from the Department of Commerce. I petitioned the Pennsylvania Census Bureau HQ to forward my records to the Homestead, Florida Census Office. They agreed to take me on if I could get my records "transferred to them in time". **That should've been a signal!**

Numerous calls to various Commerce Department functionaries couldn't make this happen for over two months. I finally found a Regional Office in Atlanta that agreed to pass them on to Florida, but "They'd have to be **"FED EX'd"** from Harrisburg, PA to Atlanta he said, where they would send them on to Homestead, Florida. Needless to say they didn't arrive in time. The actual census taking was over!

It seems that this was February, 2010 and that the Government was probably connected to the internet by then, especially since the internet was initially developed with US Federal money way back in 1963, called ARPANET — the **beginning** of today's galaxy-wide Internet.

Incident #2

I started with the Commerce Department for the Census as an hourly, expenses paid temporary employee in fall '09. I started as a volunteer with the Interior Department's National Wildlife Refuges in the summer of '10. The Interior Department required me to get a **second, duplicate security**

clearance, even though I explained that I had just been cleared by the Commerce Department. I believe these clearances were issued by separate private contractors. Why? I wonder how much each charged? Now that the Chinese have hacked the "Security Clearance" files, I guess the Chinese think there are two, cleared C3's (me twice).

Incident #3

I've been under the VA's wing for a number of years. I had a family emergency and rushed to get a 2 a.m. flight from Philadelphia to Miami. In my haste I had forgotten my daily medicines, which I get from the VA. While I was tending to my family problems in Miami I went to the VA hospital there. All I wanted to do is to get a four day supply of four different meds to hold me over till I got back home.

I had to get an appointment with a VA doctor there to approve me getting the pills I needed, none of which were narcotic. I knew my records were in the computers in the VA Hospital in Wilkes Barre, PA, because I saw the humans there hunting and pecking on them. Why did the Miami VA require a doctor visit and legions of paperwork? That data should have been instantly available on their pharmacy computers, so they could hunt and peck on them, to see my files waaaaaay up in Pennsylvania?

Here's a new one most people never consider. I've been attached to the VA's umbilical since approximately 1998 or thereabout. They determined that I was "type two" diabetic and should test my own blood-sugar level on a regular basis to make sure their prescribed meds were doing their job — and me too!

To assist in that effort the VA prescribed and supplied a glucose test meter and gave me a prescription for the necessary supplies so I could keep track of my vital glucose metric. This device was simple to use and accurate. Several years later all of a sudden I was unable to get the necessary lancets and test strips from the VA. They supplied me a new "updated" test meter, which required similar but incompatible supplies. No big deal.

Recently, again, a new meter and supplies showed up. All three of these test kits are similar in appearance and with seemingly the same, but incompatible accoutrements. Out of curiosity I tested myself with all three units which I still have, and the results were, guess what — the same!!!!

Now here's the issue, in my mind. "C" street Washington lobbyist from the Pharmaceutical industry, trying to keep their jobs, convinced or maybe coerced, or maybe sent somebody to Vegas a few times, to persuade the VA to purchase replacements for perfectly good equipment. All three of mine work great!

These seemingly insignificant sagas are all related to one or all of the following observations:

Why are lobbyist allowed anywhere near government purchasing agents — or Congress?

Why are different branches of the same Federal entity not able to connect on-line and perform as if they were all one? I should be able to get a blood test in Philadelphia in the morning and get the results, a diagnosis and a prescription in Miami that afternoon — just walk into the VA or military pharmacy there, or anywhere on earth, present my ID, pay and go. I can do that at any Wal-Mart — why not the VA?

There's layers of useless bureaucracy in the VA and **everywhere else in the whole Government,** with endless, over-regulation, each requiring other bureaucrats to massage and hunt-'n-peck.

Why wouldn't the Interior Department accept the security clearance just done by the Commerce Department? How much did each contractor charge for duplicate work? Why isn't there one agency, say Homeland Security, that provides this service for all Federal Departments? They've probably already checked me out anyway, because I refuse to be Politically Correct! I know some spook agency is poking in my computers, because anything in there referring to race or Muslims mysteriously disappears! How about that taxpayers?

Why wouldn't the personnel department in one District be able to instantly look up my records and instantly transfer an electronic copy to an authorized person somewhere else? Why does every Department's fiefdom have to have separate, but like, services?

I remember when there was a recent budget squabble between Congress and the President. There was a notice that all non-essential Departments and Services would be shut down until the budget problem was resolved. If they had remained shut down, since they were "non-essential", we would be a long way towards eliminating the national debt by now.

Wouldn't that be an interesting exercise? Make a list of all Federal **"unessential"** operations:

Energy Department — created in 1945 by Harry Truman. Why do we need that today? It seems that all they do is devise new regulations to keep American business from

exploiting American energy. They're holding up 800 miles of Keystone Pipeline when there's already 1,382,570 pipeline miles, some buried, some not in the US alone — five or six times more than the next largest producer, Russia??? There are more than 210 **natural gas pipeline <u>systems.</u>** They total more than 305,000 miles of pipe. The rest are some form of petroleum or its refined products.[8]

Nations have been using pipelines worldwide forever, to transport everything from coal slurry to milk and even beer. So, EPA and Obama, quit politicking and get out of the way of the Keystone and move on to something more important, and less political.

Education Department — President Regan

campaigned I believe, on eliminating this department altogether. He did succeed in cutting it back considerably, but over time it's grown again. This administration has tried to focus on quantifying teachers by measuring students. Reportedly the trend is to teach to the test, ensuring teacher's pathway to Tenure.

If measured by statistics alone, the whole Education Department should lose its tenure tomorrow! This effort is a failure today and probably should acquiesce to local control — State, County, Township and Church. That seemed to work well, for many years. There are many worldwide polls on such subjects and the US ranks 17 out of 55 nations in one interesting study.[9]

Interior Department — Manages about 20% of

the US land mass including dams, waterways, Federal parks,

Wildlife Preserves and landmarks. It regulates use of these areas, reportedly for the Public Good. It also seems they collude with the Energy Department to preclude use of Public Lands for energy exploitation, forcing us to seek resources from other parts of the world, like OPEC for instance.

IRS - Internal Revenue Service — Created to collect the taxes donated by us, and also created by a Democratic Congress and signed into law by Democrat President Woodrow Wilson, then ratified in 1913 by the 16th amendment to the Constitution. Long considered to be the most hated government entity, due to its annual April 15th fleecing of the electorate and its flagrant use in recent times as a political tool, has further enhanced its low standing. There are many proposals to downsize or eliminate this Department altogether. Eliminating loopholes, tax shelters and adding graduated flat tax rates seems to be gathering acceptance.

Labor Department — It was originally created to eliminate unfair treatment, unsafe and underpaid working conditions and present a unified voice in dealing with business Management. The pendulum has swung way too far left and is now beginning to settle somewhere in the middle. Right to Work laws are beginning to make Unions offer more to the worker than to Union Management.

Army Corps of Engineers — 37,000 mostly civilian employees who provide design and construction expertise for Federal Projects. Originally a US Army creation by George Washington, they are generally absorbed with Continental US projects under the control of the Interior Department, but not always. The technical aspects of the Corps should be absorbed into the Interior Department.

Environmental Protection Agency — Over 15,000 mostly technical positions. This is not a Cabinet Level Department, but it has the responsibility for technical management of America's environment, a **regulatory agency** only, with **w i d e** environmental powers that sometimes seeks to operate without any leash on its efforts.

They have done many notable things in the name of clean environment, but rather than regulating businesses out of business, should be helping them resolve issues with innovative and specific solutions.

A good case in point is the decades long regulatory effort to help clean up car and truck emissions. They didn't put people out of business, but worked with business to solve those vexing problems by **easing into** restrictive plateaus, rather than "It's this way, or else. Do it now," as seems to be the current approach.

City-wide smog (usually caused by car & truck exhaust emissions) is mostly **gone** in this country now, thanks to the past combined efforts of Environmentalist, Business and Government. To toot my horn, my philosophy of "Make a good flexible plan" solved that problem to everyone's benefit it seems.

I remember one morning, being in Los Angeles on business in the late 60's when I went outside my hotel and wasn't able to see the red traffic-lights at each end of the block — just one city block! The smog was so thick you could see, smell and taste it. Your eyes would burn and weep because of it!

Those entities must still be on the side of Americans as well as the "snail darters", etc., etc., etc.. Apparently, current thinking is still lopsided and favoring the fish without considering all aspects of the problem equally. The current California drought is affecting more than just some environmentalist wet dreams. We've already had a "Dust Bowl" or two and should have had a more flexible plan with contingencies — the problem isn't fully solved is it? Keep going.

The EPA overreach has just been enhanced by a new pile of regulations, a bigger pile than Obama Care. They're trying to govern every drop of water on our part of the planet. If you have a puddle in your back yard, you can't even piss in it! They're trying to make cows stand in line to use Porta-Potties.

The current California drought is threatening to put agriculture in general there, out of business in favor of the "Snail Darter".[10] It seems that ill-conceived plans, which result in lopsided regulations and over-zealous regulators with tunnel vision, are just one of the major reason this whole country is on the verge of suffering a nervous breakdown.

The Endangered Species Act of the late 1970's probably should have considered everything that might be endangered if enacted, back then and now in this century. It should've included California's Agriculture Industry and its way of life as well as the Snail Darters! Environmentalist' lobbying, in the current ongoing California case, should have induced Congress to plan to mitigate the possible effects of a drought in that area as well as protect "That stupid little fish" as one politician posited. Has anyone considered desalinization? If so, where is it?

Over regulation has, maybe, been slowed by the recent Supreme Court decision to require impact statements (How Much $$$$?) with each new regulation. Further control is needed to mitigate over regulation, by requiring Congressional approval of each and every new dictate and a review of the whole regulatory library every four years for instance.

Regulation writers are creating regulations and enforcing them as if they were laws — without any oversight! That's got to stop. Congress creates the laws.

Combine Interior, Energy, Army Corps of Engineers and the EPA. These Departments and Agencies all have missions relating to this patch of Earth we inhabit, called America. They're charged with managing the land, the air over it and what's under it. Let them work together to make it compatible with humans too. Maybe we'll just have to eat all these critters they're trying to protect.

National Science Foundation

NASA

National Institute of Health

These are all related to science in one form or another. Why not combine 'everything science and research' into one entity where cross pollination of thought might be beneficial rather than "Not Invented Here" separatism and bureaucracy getting in the way.

Create a Science Pentagon, where pure research and academic study grant-programs are directed and funded and applied research into space programs, environmental programs and new energy and medical solutions are developed by funding industry research — all together in one place so they can talk together, all use the same secretary and copier — go to the same johns and the same five o'clock bar.

Small Business Administration

Corp. for National & Community Service

Bureaucrats Ad-Finitum

I began to scour the internet for facts and figures relating to the numerous US Agencies, Commissions, Departments, etc., and was amazed at the width and breadth of government control over everything imaginable. Each of the hundreds of offices have, in some way, control over you and me. Each has its staff of bureaucrats that are similar, managing a bigger staff of bureaucrats, keeping track of some obscure bits of information regarding **their role in your affairs.** The following pages are derived from Wikipedia's lists of Government Offices. I'm sure I've left out a few million "Non Essential" bureaucrats, all "Regulation" writers and enforcers of some kind.

Keep in mind that listings in the following pages are just some portion of the huge number of employees we support who all love the security of their jobs and the top shelf benefits — for life. I don't blame them. So would I. These lists don't include contractors. Maybe the Bureaucrats should be phased out and just keep all the contractors??

Please peruse the following lists and imagine if you will, that each office must have a **Big Boss**, and numerous littler bosses, all with secretaries and an office staff to man (person) the copiers, supplies ordering, Christmas party, etc., etc., etc.. There's probably also a level 20 person whose job it is, is to make sure everybody in the group fully complies with all regulations and follows all new "Politically Correct" edicts.

This person is also allowed to correct underlings personally, for a personal favorite, incorrect thought uttered in a **"Return to the good old days" slip of the tongue**. This person is in charge of the "Best New Regulation of the Year Contest". The winner gets a full week, all expenses paid, to Caesars' Palace — hot tub, wine and all!

Scan the following list (incomplete) to see if we really need all of this. It is printed here from Wikipedia statistics and is only generalities, to help illustrate the breadth and depth of the tumor. It's unbelievable!

Did you know there are 465 + Agencies, frequently referred to as the "Shadow Fourth Branch" of the US Federal Government. These are mostly independent and not answerable directly to any of the other three branches.

Almost Autonomous!

Have you wondered how they seem to operate without answering to Congress — how they create endless regulation while we all wonder, "Who's watching the hen-house?" US citizens have two Senators and our local Congressman who can't regulate these 465 + enclaves of rulemaking humanoids for us — so they mostly operate autonomously. Seems to me that has to change in our reorganization of this "out of control mess".

I have included, for your reading pleasure and amusement, just a few pages of out-of-control bureaucracy. I hope this list amazes you as much as it did me. It is by no means a scientific or official list but gathered by me from Wikipedia and poking around on the internet. My intent is to impress you with how we are being over managed and over taxed to pay for all this, most of which we don't need or want. [11] ....

 Check to **KEEP** because it is <u>**ESSENTIAL!**</u>

S If you would move to State Control.

N "Nice to Have"

X Who cares about that?

	DEPARTMENT- AGENCY - COMMISSION
	Independent & Gov't. Owned Corps.
	Federal Election Commission
	National Archives and Records Admin.
	Office of the Federal Register
	Office of Government Ethics
	Office of Personnel Management
	Federal Executive Institute
	Combined Federal Campaign
	Office of Special Counsel
	Federal Trade Commission
	Consumer Product Safety Commission
	Federal Housing Finance Agency
	Federal Housing Finance Board
	Institute of Museum and Library Svcs.
	International Broadcasting Bureau
	National Constitution Center
	National Endowment for the Arts

	DEPARTMENT- AGENCY - COMMISSION
	National Endowment for Humanities
	National Aeronautics & Space Admin.
	National Science Foundation
	United States Antarctic Program
	United States Arctic Program
	Nuclear Regulatory Commission
	Alaska Natural Gas Transp. Proj.
	Tennessee Valley Authority
	African Development Foundation
	Export-Import Bank of the US
	Inter-American Foundation
	Overseas Private Investment Corp.
	US Agency for Int'l Development
	Advisory Council Historic Preservation
	Environmental Protection Agency
	Federal Labor Relations Authority
	Federal Mediation & Conciliation Svc.
	Fed. Mine Safety-Health Rev. Comm.
	Nat'l Labor Relations Board - NLRB
	National Mediation Board
	Occupational Safety-Health Review
	Office of Compliance
	Commodity Futures Trading Comm.
	Farm Credit Administration
	Federal Reserve System
	U S Consumer Fin. Protec. Bureau
	Federal Deposit Insurance Corporation
	National Credit Union Administration

	DEPARTMENT- AGENCY - COMMISSION
	Central Liquidity Facility
	Securities and Exchange Commission
	Securities Investor Protection Corp.
	Small Business Administration
	Military Postal Service Agency
	Postal Regulatory Commission
	United States Postal Service
	Armed Forces Retirement Home
	Fed. Retirement Thrift Investment Bd.
	Pension Benefit Guaranty Corporation
	Railroad Retirement Board
	Social Security Administration
	Offender Supervision Agency
	General Services Administration
	National Capital Planning Commission
	Amtrak (National RR Passenger Corp.)
	Federal Maritime Commission
	National Transportation Safety Board
	Corp. for Nat'l & Community Service
	Peace Corps
	Central Intelligence Agency
	Defense Nuclear Facilities Safety Bd.
	National Counterintelligence Exec.
	Director of National Intelligence
	Intelligence Advanced Research Proj.
	Selective Service System
	Commission on Civil Rights
	Equal Employment Opportunity Comm.

	DEPARTMENT- AGENCY - COMMISSION
	National Council on Disability
	Quasi-Official Agencies
	Legal Services Corporation
	Smithsonian Institution
	J F K Center for the Performing Arts
	State Justice Institute
	United States Institute of Peace
	National Trust for Historic Preservation
	Brand USA
	Graduate School USA
	Architect of the Capitol
	United States Botanic Garden
	Congressional Budget Office
	Government Accountability Office
	Government Printing Office
	Library of Congress
	Congressional Research Service
	United States Copyright Office
	Office of Compliance
	United States Capitol Guide Service
	United States Capitol Police
	Judicial branch
	Administrative Office of the U S Courts
	Federal Judicial Center
	Judicial Conference of the US
	Office of Probation and Pretrial Svcs.
	United States Sentencing Commission

	DEPARTMENT- AGENCY - COMMISSION
	Executive Branch
	Asst. to the President & Chief of Staff
	Council of Economic Advisers
	Council on Environmental Quality
	Domestic Policy Council
	National Economic Council
	National Security Council
	Office of Communications
	Office of Administration
	Office of Management and Budget
	Office of National Drug Control Policy
	Public Engagement & Intergov.
	Office of the Senior Advisor to POTUS
	Office of Science and Tech. Policy
	Office of the First Lady
	Office of the President
	Office of the Vice President
	Office of the White House Counsel
	President's Intelligence Advisory Board
	President's Intelligence Oversight Bd.
	Trade Representative
	White House Office
	White House Military Office
	Agriculture Department
	Agricultural Marketing Service
	Agricultural Research Service

	DEPARTMENT- AGENCY - COMMISSION
	Animal and Plant Health Inspec. Svc.
	Center for Nutrition Policy & Promotion
	Economic Research Service
	Farm Service Agency
	Commodity Credit Corporation
	Food and Nutrition Service
	Food Safety and Inspection Service
	Foreign Agricultural Service
	Forest Service
	Grain Packers & Stockyards Admin.
	Marketing and Regulatory Programs
	National Agricultural Statistics Service
	National Institute of Food & Agriculture
	4-H
	Natural Resources Conservation Svc.
	Risk Management Agency
	Federal Crop Insurance Corporation
	Rural Business and Coop. Programs
	Office of Rural Development
	Research, Education and Economics
	Rural Housing Service
	Rural Utilities Service
	Commerce Department
	Bureau of Economic Analysis
	Bureau of Industry and Security
	Census Bureau
	Economic Development Administration

	DEPARTMENT- AGENCY - COMMISSION
	Economics & Statistics Administration
	Export Enforcement
	Import Administration
	International Trade Administration
	Office of Travel and Tourism Industry
	Invest in America
	Manufacturing and Services
	Marine and Aviation Operations
	Market Access and Compliance
	Minority Business Dev. Agency
	Nat'l Oceanic & Atmospheric Admin.
	NOAA Commissioned Corps
	Nat'l Environ. Satellite Data Info. Svc
	National Marine Fisheries Service
	National Oceanic Service
	National Weather Service
	Nat'l Telecom & Information Admin.
	Patent and Trademark Office
	Nat'l Institute of Standards & Tech.
	National Technical Information Service
	Trade Promo U S & Foreign Com. Svc.
	Defense Department
	Department of the Army
	United States Army
	Army Intelligence & Security Command
	Army Corps of Engineers

DEPARTMENT- AGENCY - COMMISSION	
	Department of the Navy
	United States Navy
	Office of Naval Intelligence
	U.S. Naval Academy
	Marine Corps
	Marine Corps Intelligence Activity
	Department of the Air Force
	United States Air Force
	Civil Air Patrol
	USAF Intel, Surveillance & Recon.
	Joint Chiefs of Staff
	National Guard Bureau
	Air National Guard
	Army National Guard
	Defense Adv. Research Proj. Agency
	Defense Commissary Agency
	Defense Contract Audit Agency
	Defense Contract Mgmt. Agency
	Defense Finance and Accounting Svc.
	Defense Information Systems Agency
	Defense Intelligence Agency
	Defense Clandestine Service
	Defense Logistics Agency
	Defense Security Cooperation Agency
	Defense Security Service
	Defense Technical Information Center
	Defense Threat Reduction Agency
	Missile Defense Agency

DEPARTMENT- AGENCY - COMMISSION	
	National Security Agency
	Central Security Service
	National Reconnaissance Office
	National Geospatial-Intel. Agency
	Naval Criminal Investigative Service
	Pentagon Force Protection Agency
	United States Pentagon Police
	American Forces Information Service
	Defense POW/Missing Personnel Off.
	Dept. of Defense Education Activity
	DOD Dependents Schools
	Defense Human Resources Activity
	Office of Economic Adjustment
	TRICARE Management Activity
	Washington Headquarters Services
	West Point Military Academy
Education Department	
	Office of Communications & Outreach
	Office of the General Counsel (OGC)
	Office of Inspector General
	Office of Legislation & Cong. Affairs
	Office for Civil Rights (OCR)
	Office of Educ. Technology (OET)
	Institute of Education Sciences (IES)
	Nat'l Center for Education Statistics
	Nat'l Assessment of Educ.Progress
	Education Resources Info. Center

	DEPARTMENT- AGENCY - COMMISSION
	Office of Innovation and Improvement
	Office of the Chief Financial Officer
	Office of Management
	Office of the Chief Information Officer
	Office of Planning, Evaluation & Policy
	Budget Service
	Postsecondary Education (OPE) Off.
	Office of Vocational and Adult Ed.
	Office of Federal Student Aid (FSA)
	Advisory Bd. on Tribal Colleges
	Advisory Bd. on Black Colleges
	Office of Elementary & Secondary Ed.
	Office of Migrant Education (OME)
	Office of Safe and Healthy Students
	School Achievement & Accountability
	Asian Americans Pacific Islanders Init.
	Amer. Indian Alaska Native Initiative
	Hispanic Educ. Excellence Initiative
	Educ. African Americans Initiative
	Limited English Student Achievement
	Special Ed. & Rehabilitative Svcs.
	Disability and Rehabilitation Research
	Office of Special Education Programs
	Rehabilitation Services Administration
	Office of Innovation and Improvement
	Advisory Councils and Committees
	National Assessment Governing Bd.
	Nat'l Advisory Council on Indian Educ.

DEPARTMENT- AGENCY - COMMISSION	
	Federal Interagency Comm. on Educ.
	Advisory Comm. Disabled Students
	National Board for Education Sciences
	Postsecondary Ed. Improvement Fund
	Gallaudet University
	Howard University
	National Technical Inst. for the Deaf
US Department of Energy	
	Energy Information Administration
	Federal Energy Regulatory Comm.
	National Laboratories & Tech. Centers
	Univ. Corp. for Atmospheric Research
	National Nuclear Security Admin.
	Power Marketing Administrations
	Bonneville Power Administration
	Southeastern Power Administration
	Western Area Power Administration
US Dept. of Health and Human Services — HHS	
	Administration on Aging
	Admin. for Children Youth & Families
	Healthcare Research & Quality Agency
	Ctrs. for Disease Control & Prevention
	CDC Foundation
	Inst. for Occupational Safety & Health
	Epidemic Intelligence Service
	National Center for Health Statistics

	DEPARTMENT- AGENCY - COMMISSION
	Medicare and Medicaid Svcs. Centers
	Food and Drug Administration
	Reagan-Udall Foundation
	Health Resources & Services Admin.
	Patient Affordable Healthcare Act
	Independent Payment Advisory Board
	Indian Health Service
	National Institutes of Health
	National Institute of Mental Health
	Public Health Service
	Federal Occupational Health
	Office of the Surgeon General
	US Public Health Svc. Corps
	Drug Abuse, Mental Health Admin.
	Homeland Security
	Fed. Emergency Management Agency
	FEMA Corps
	U.S. Fire Administration
	National Flood Insurance Program
	Federal Law Enforcement Training Ctr.
	Transportation Security Administration
	US Citizenship and Immigration Svcs.
	United States Coast Guard
	Coast Guard Intelligence
	National Ice Center
	United States Ice Patrol
	US Customs & Border Protection

DEPARTMENT - AGENCY - COMMISSION	
	Office of Air and Marine
	Office of Border Patrol
	U.S. Border Patrol
	Office of Field Operations
	US Immigration & Customs Enforce.
	Enforcement and Removal Operations
	Homeland Security Investigations
	Office of Professional Responsibility
	United States Secret Service
	Domestic Nuclear Detection Office
	Office of Health Affairs
	Office of Component Services
	Int'l Affairs & Global Health Sec. Office
	Office of Medical Readiness
	Office of WMD and Biodefense
	Office of Intelligence and Analysis
	Office of Operations Coordination
	Office of Policy
	Homeland Security Advisory Council
	Office of International Affairs
	Office of Immigration Statistics
	Office of Policy Development
	Office for State & Local Law Enforce.
	Office of Strategic Plans
	Private Sector Office
	Directorate for Management
	Nat'l. Protection & Prog. Directorate
	Federal Protective Service

DEPARTMENT- AGENCY - COMMISSION	
	Cyber Sec. & Communications Office
	National Communications System
	National Cyber Security Division
	US Computer Emer. Readiness Team
	Office of Emergency Communications
	Office of Infrastructure Protection
	Office of Risk Management & Analysis
	Visitor & Immigrant Status Indic. Tech.
	Science and Technology Directorate
	Environmental Measurements Lab
	National Urban Security Tech. Lab
	Homeland Security ARPA
	Office of Research
	Office of National Laboratories
	Office of University Programs
	Counter IED Office
	Office of Transition
	Commercialization Office
	Long Range Broad Agency Office
	Product Transition Office
	Safety Act Office
	Technology Transfer Office
	Border and Maritime Security Division
	Chemical and Biological Division
	Command, Control & Interop. Division
	Explosives Division
	Human Factors Division
	Infrastructure/Geophysical Division

DEPARTMENT- AGENCY - COMMISSION
Business Operations Division
Executive Secretariat Office
Human Capital Office
Key Security Office
Office of Chief Administrative Officer
Office of the Chief Information Officer
Planning and Management
Corporate Communications Division
Interagency & 1st Responders Prog.
Int'l. Cooperative Programs Office
Operations Analysis Division
Homeland Security Studies & Analysis
Homeland Security Sys. Eng. & Dev.
Policy and Budget Division
Special Programs Division
Test & Evaluation and Standards Div.
Housing & Urban Development - HUD
Federal Housing Administration
Federal Housing Finance Agency
Center for Faith-Based Partnerships
Departmental Enforcement Center
Office of Community Planning & Dev.
Congress & Intergov. Relations Off.
Office of Equal Emp.Opportunity
Office of Fair Housing and Equal Opp.
Office of Field Policy and Management
Office of the General Counsel

	DEPARTMENT- AGENCY - COMMISSION
	Healthy Homes & Lead Hazards Office
	Office of Hearings and Appeals
	Office of Labor Relations
	Office of Policy Dev. and Research
	Office of Public Affairs
	Office of Public and Indian Housing
	Disadvantaged Business Utilization
	Sustainable Housing and Communities
	Gov. Nat'l Mortg. Assoc. (Ginnie Mae)
	United States Dept. of the Interior
	Bureau of Indian Affairs
	Bureau of Land Management
	Bureau of Ocean Energy Management
	Bureau of Reclamation
	Safety & Environment Enforcement
	Fish and Wildlife Service
	National Park Service
	Office of Insular Affairs
	Office of Surface Mining
	National Mine Map Repository
	United States Geological Survey
	Justice Department
	Antitrust Division
	Asset Forfeiture Program
	BATF & Explosives
	Civil Division

DEPARTMENT- AGENCY - COMMISSION	
	Civil Rights Division
	Community Oriented Policing Services
	Community Relations Service
	Criminal Division
	Diversion Control Program
	Drug Enforcement Administration
	Environment & Natural Resources Div.
	Exec. Office for Immigration Review
	Crime Drug Enforcement Task Force
	Executive Office for US Attorneys
	Executive Office for US Trustees
	FBI — Federal Bureau of Investigation
	Federal Bureau of Prisons
	UNICOR
	Foreign Claims Settlement Comm.
	INTERPOL - US National Central Bur.
	Justice Management Division
	National Crime Information Center
	National Drug Intelligence Center
	National Institute of Corrections
	National Security Division
	Office of Associate Attorney General
	Office of the Attorney General
	Attorney Recruitment & Mgmt. Office
	Office of the Chief Information Officer
	Office of the Deputy Attorney General
	Office of Dispute Resolution
	Office of the Federal Detention Trustee

	DEPARTMENT- AGENCY - COMMISSION
	Office of Information Policy
	Office of Intergov. Public Liaison
	Office of Intelligence and Analysis
	Office of Justice Programs
	Bureau of Justice Assistance
	Bureau of Justice Statistics
	Community Capacity Dev. Office
	Nat'l Criminal Justice Reference Svc.
	National Institute of Justice
	Juvenile Justice & Delinquency Prev.
	Office for Victims of Crime
	Office of Legal Counsel
	Office of Legal Policy
	Office of Legislative Affairs
	Office of the Pardon Attorney
	Office of Privacy and Civil Liberties
	Office of Professional Responsibility
	Office of Public Affairs
	Office of Sex Offender Affairs
	Office of the Solicitor General
	Office of Special Counsel
	Office of Tribal Justice
	Office on Violence Against Women
	Pro. Responsibility Advisory Office
	Tax Division
	United States Attorneys
	United States Marshals
	United States Parole Commission

	DEPARTMENT- AGENCY - COMMISSION
	United States Trustee Program
	Labor **Department**
	Bureau of International Labor Affairs
	Bureau of Labor Statistics
	Faith-Based & Neighborhood Partners
	Employee Benefits Security Admin.
	Employment and Training Admin.
	Job Corps
	Mine Safety and Health Administration
	Occupational Safety & Health Admin.
	Veterans' Employment & Training Svc.
	Wage & Hour Division - Women's Bur.
	Administrative Review Board
	Benefits Review Board
	Employees' Comp. Appeals Bd.
	Office of Administrative Law Judges
	Asst. Secretary for Admin. & Mgmt.
	Office of the Assistant Seciy. for Policy
	Office of the Chief Information Officer
	Congressional & Intergov. Affairs
	Office of Disability Employment Policy
	Federal Contract Compliance Prog.
	Labor-Management Standards Office
	Office of the Solicitor
	Office of Worker's Compensation Pgm.
	Energy Emp. Occup. Illness Comp.
	Wirtz Labor Library

DEPARTMENT- AGENCY - COMMISSION		
State Department		
	Nat'l Council for the Traditional Arts	
	Bureau of Legislative Affairs	
	Office of the Legal Adviser	
	Executive Secretariat	
	Office of the Chief of Protocol	
	Office for Civil Rights	
	Coordinator for Counterterrorism	
	United States Global AIDS Coordinator	
	Office of Global Criminal Justice	
	Policy Planning Staff	
	Bureau of Political-Military Affairs	
	Weapons Removal and Abatement	
	Arms Control, Verification & Comp.	
	Democracy, Human Rights, and Labor	
	Oceans, Environ. & Scientific Affairs	
	Population, Refugees, & Migration	
	Monitor Trafficking in Persons	
	Economic Bureau - Energy & Business	
	Bureau of Administration	
	Bureau of Consular Affairs	
	Office of Overseas Citizens Services	
	Bureau of Diplomatic Security	
	Diplomatic Security Service	
	Office of Foreign Missions	
	Overseas Security Advisory Council	
	Bureau of Human Resources	

DEPARTMENT- AGENCY - COMMISSION	
	Family Liaison Office
	Information Resource Management
	Bureau of Overseas Buildings Ops.
	Bureau of Resource Management
	Foreign Service Institute
	Mgmt. Policy, Rightsizing & Innovation
	Bureau of East Asian & Pacific Affairs
	Bureau of African Affairs
	Bureau of European & Eurasian Affairs
	Internat. Narc. & Law Enforc. Affairs
	Bureau of International Org. Affairs
	Bureau of Near Eastern Affairs
	Bureau of Asian Affairs
	Bureau of Western Hemisphere Affairs
	Bureau of Educ. & Cultural Affairs
	Bureau of International Info Pgms.
	Bureau of Public Affairs
	Office of the Historian
	Policy, Plan. & Diplomacy Resources
	US Mission to European Agencies
	U S Mission to Int'l Orgs. in Vienna
	US Mission to the African Union
	United States Mission to ASEAN
	US mission to the Arab League
	US mission to the Council of Europe
	US Mission to the European Union
	Mission to Int'l Civil Aviation Org.
	United States Mission to NATO

DEPARTMENT- AGENCY - COMMISSION
Economic Co-op. Org. & Development
U S Mission to OAS
Mission to Europe Security & Coop.
US Mission to the United Nations
US Mission to UN Rome Agencies
U N Office & Int'l Orgs. in Geneva
U N Educ., Scientific, Cultural Orgs.
U N Envir. Prog. & Human Settlements
In addition to the departments listed above the State Department has 173 Embassies worldwide with 127 associated supporting Consular offices — i.e., Benghazzi.
Transportation Department
Bureau of Transportation Statistics
Federal Aviation Administration
Air Traffic Organization
Federal Highway Administration
Federal Motor Carrier Safety Admin.
Federal Railroad Administration
Federal Transit Administration
Maritime Administration
National Highway Traffic Safety Admin.
Intelligence, Security & Emer. Resp.
Pipeline & Hazardous Materials Safety
Research Innovative Tech. Admin.
St. Lawrence Seaway System

	DEPARTMENT- AGENCY - COMMISSION
	Saint Lawrence Seaway Dev. Corp.
	St. Lawrence Seaway Dev. Corp.
	Surface Transportation Board
	Alcohol-Tobacco Tax & Trade Bureau
	Bureau of Engraving and Printing
	Bureau of the Fiscal Service
	Comm. Dev. Financial Inst. Fund
	Federal Consulting Group
	Financial Crimes Enforcement Network
	Internal Revenue Service
	Office of the Comptroller of Currency
	Office of Thrift Supervision
	Office of Financial Stability
	United States Mint
	Office of Domestic Finance
	Office of Economic Policy
	Office of International Affairs
	Office of Tax Policy
	Office of Terrorism & Financial Intel.
	Treasurer of the United States
Veterans Affairs	
	National Cemetery Administration
	Veterans Benefits Administration
	Veterans Health Administration
	Board of Veterans' Appeals
	Faith-Based and Community Initiatives
	Center for Minority Veterans

		DEPARTMENT- AGENCY - COMMISSION
		Center for Veterans Enterprise
		Center for Women Veterans
		Office of Advisory Committee Mgmt.
		Discrimination Complaint Adjudication
		Office of Survivors Assistance
		Disadvantaged Business Utilization
		Veterans Service Org. Liaison
		Independent Government Entities & Acts
		COMSAT
		American Institute in Taiwan
		Cotton Incorporated
		Dairy Management Inc.
		In-Q-Tel
		Protestant Episcopal Cathedral Found.
		Washington National Cathedral
		Financial Industry Regulatory Authority
		National Consumer Cooperative Bank
		Nat'l Corp. for Housing Partnerships
		National Endowment for Democracy
		National Fish and Wildlife Foundation
		Nat'l Technical Institute for the Deaf
		Neighborhood Reinvestment Corp.
		Pennsylvania Ave. Dev. Corporation
		The Financing Corporation
		Sister Cities International
		Twin Cities International
		US Olympic Comm. (also chartered)

DEPARTMENT- AGENCY - COMMISSION	
	US National Paralympic Committee
	United States Anti-Doping Agency

Lobbyist

And just think — every one of the preceding offices, agencies and departments have legions of Washington's "K" Street lobbyists (12,000+ who are legally registered and many thousands more not registered at all), all earning big bucks by inviting our Legislators and Bureaucrats to their Saturday barbeques — some of which, I'll bet, are even in Vegas, Dubai or Rio!

There's much controversy over elected officials being bought by donations to campaign funds, or with illegal gifts or promises of cushy jobs — after Congress. To be fair to their efforts, most of these complex issues brought before Congress are beyond the intimate understanding of legislators and therefore lobbyists, pro and con, can and do educate them.

It seems however, that most of the educating today is done behind closed doors or at the nearest barroom and to just the most influential legislators who herd or intimidate their uninformed colleagues to "get in line".

Why not mandate that the "Educating" be done only to the House, and only during quarterly "Omnibus" sessions where Amicus briefs are presented on each issue by lobbyists, before voting. Isn't this how the Supreme Court is managed?

Once a new bill gets through the House it passes to the Senate where no lobbyist, their campaign fund gifts, or coercion should ever be allowed access. After due deliberation without "K" Street meddling, the new bill's individual items are passed or rejected, then forwarded for the President's approval in total.

There are many nice-to-have Agencies, Departments, Offices, Corporations, Internationals, Institutes, Foundations, Endowments, Cooperatives, Authorities, Liaisons, Initiatives, Affairs, etc., ad nauseam. They all receive endowments, funds and grants annually, right out of our pockets — all of whom scramble each year for more of our Chinese money.

I don't mean to lay off all these Americans, but there's just too many, too much duplication, too many "Nice to Have" functions, too many onerous regulations and zealous "gov'mint men" orgasmic over sticking it to low-life, non-Gov'mint Americans.

A former US President (??) was charged at one time with reshaping the structure of the whole government. I believe George Bush and Barak Obama and most all former Presidents made overtures along these lines, but nothing ever happens, because its mostly campaign rhetoric and it says so on the teleprompter.

I believe the cadre of Department and Agency heads throughout the government were and are mostly former lobbyist. We need that kind of re-do **now**. Assign a notable, forward thinking Libertarian to that task.[12]

Maybe that's an important endeavor for the new Vice President to manage. It seems he doesn't usually have much to do. I'm sure he can fit that task into his busy schedule. The new Veep needs a serious job.

If I had the job, I think I'd create three "Pentagon-like" facilities and group all functions there. The Judicial, Legislative and Executive Branches can stay the same, but all other Federal functionaries should be grouped and consolidated into broad general categories.

For instance, the existing Pentagon would contain all Defense and Intelligence functions under one roof, reporting to Congress. All military, State Department, Homeland Security, NSA, CIA, Coast Guard, Space Agencies, FBI, BATF, Border Patrol and Secret Service would be consolidated into one entity. Yeah — why not? Everyone's a uniformed warrior or a secret agent.

The second Pentagon would deal entirely with management of the American continent and everything that happens on it, under and over it. The Interior, Environment, Commerce, Labor, Energy, Education, Health and Rehabilitation, Birth to Death Entitlements, WPA, Agriculture, EPA, etc..

The Third Pentagon would manage all support functions for the American Economy — Federal Reserve, Mint, Treasury and IRS. They would provide all Federal communications, Internet.Gov, software development, testing and management, security archives, **all separate and protected from the world's current internet.**

How Do We Do That?

To begin this grand overhaul, the first step would be to initiate a force-reduction through "Early-Out" retirements, mandatory hiring freezes in **all** departments and agencies — management, administrative and backup functions included, except military, intelligence and Boots-On-The-Ground.

The intention here is not to lay off Federal employees, but to eliminate the notion that you can't get fired — sort of like "No Government Tenure", and to encourage early out retirements. Can you imagine the infighting and squabbling if we could bring that off within the whole Federal workforce which is way too top heavy today.

I was part of a large Corporate merger in the computer world of the mid 1980's. When, after it was all over in 1986, there were 200 Vice Presidents and 600 Directors. I was one of the 600!

There were 150,000 employees combined worldwide at the start of the merger, and today only 35,000. It was ill conceived and not well thought out — **no long range plan maybe?** Just now, 20 years later they've managed to finally combine their operating systems into a single computing architecture — TWENTY YEARS LATER! The CEO who managed this Corporate disaster was an ex **Federal Department Head** under Jimmy Carter. No wonder!

Some beginning moves to start the Federal process today maybe — eliminate all face to face meetings requiring travel, room and board. Replace all meetings with teleconferences — no travel for conventions, conferences, and certainly political efforts etc.. Eliminate "First-Class" airfare and **all bonuses and**

financial incentives. Federal salaries are generally higher than Civilian salaries. Institute a wage freeze until parity with non-union civilian wages is achieved.

Ensure all benefits are universal and equal with normal Americans. Reduce per-deim for required overnight travel to $200 per day for every government worker — elected, appointed or anointed.

If $200 times the number of Federal passengers onboard Air Force One isn't enough to get it off the ground, take freight too! Never use it for political trips unless paid for by the hiring party. Use the bus or choo-choo more often.

The hiring freeze will remain in effect until the deficit is eliminated — until the rainy-day fund is solvent, and the US annual "Zero-based" budget is balanced. It automatically goes back into effect if any of these annual requirements are not met.

Until these goals are achieved, there should be no "Foreign Aid" and deferred support payments to the UN and NATO. In fact maybe the US might levy a per person daily allowance to the UN & NATO for all military aid?? I think Trump agrees with me on this one.

Most will agree these are harsh and Draconian measures, but once started, the world might imagine how serious the US is about regaining and ensuring its top position. We can fund anything we want if our deficit is gone, the "Rainy-Day" fund is full, and our annual budget is always zero-balanced.

EVERYBODY WORKS!

Recently, while visiting some of my kids who live in Philadelphia, I decided that it was time to get the engine oil in my Jeep renewed. I went to what I thought used to be a Jiffy Lube I had used before, but was now closed partially, due to the owner's passing. One of the former employees had set up shop there trying to reestablish the business.

The work was professionally done in short order, partially augmented by at least three unemployed millenials, all vying for any chance to get in good with the new boss. These were not ghetto people who had long ago given up on a job, but they were today's twenty somethings who are on the verge of giving up. All were hoping for a chance to earn a ten-spot, but mostly getting in the way. I still had to remind them they'd forgotten the "L" part of LOF (Lube, Oil & Filter).

There was something missing — something sad in their faces. They were listless — all were drab and in the shadows, with no particular skills or apparent long term choices or chances. I was down that day myself, having been closer to current reality than I had been before — it wasn't like it was in my youth. You could get three jobs every day if you wanted to walk that far — but, not now.

How do we fix that?

Certainly not by saying, "**Well — go get on welfare. You won't have to work**". That's what we say today. Nice 1950's neighborhoods have turned to ghettos full of the "other people" who've already given up, or never knew anything better. They don't contribute, but absorb whatever largess can be mooched from society or their parents. Sadly, most never return to become useful citizens — others are on the verge of joining their ranks without some hope on the horizon. There's not much now. I was in the midst of three that day, mid March 2015.

I watched the Baltimore Millenials till midnight 4/28/2015, and all the next day. Although their skin color is different they are the "other people" too.

I remember celebrating my 32nd birthday, July 24 1967, as "other people" burned parts of Detroit city down too — all around me! Everyone in the Belcrest hotel on Seward Street spent the evening of July 23rd huddled on the roof of that hotel, watching the fires begin to encircle it.

I eventually went to bed that night, but awoke about 2 a.m. the next morning — that birthday morning, to the rumbling of a tank not 20 feet from my second floor bedroom window. I could have reached out from my bed and almost touch it. The National Guard and the 82nd Airborne were both in attendance that morn. A block or two further down that alley was the back of a motel where some "other people" where holed-up, shooting at the police. I believe the tank reversed the course of that confrontation. I went back to sleep about 4 a.m. that 32nd birthday morn.

How Did Roosevelt's "New Deal" Fix Problems In His Era?

"FDR came into office in 1933 with no clear or specific plan for what to do in the middle of the depression. He was known to say **"Try something. If it doesn't work try something else."** He and his advisors recognized that they must at least, try to do something!

"These attempts gave Americans the hope that something was being done. Roosevelt's basic philosophy of economics became known as the three **"R's"** of Relief, Recovery and Reform. The programs created to meet these goals generated jobs and most importantly, **hope**. They also generated a series of acts and agencies that created a huge federal bureaucracy.

"The New Deal"

What did Roosevelt mean by relief, recovery and reform?

Relief - Immediate action taken to halt the economy's further deterioration.

Recovery - Temporary programs to restart consumer demand.

Reform - Programs to insure citizens against economic disasters".[13]

Most of FDR's **Reforms** are still in existence today, albeit modernized occasionally. Some new form of his original **Relief & Recovery** is needed today. President Obama's "Shovel Ready Jobs" approach sounded good in the beginning and did indeed seem to be a good start, but it was **hampered by the government's own over-regulation**. Na na na na naaaaaa na!

I believe the first two FDR platforms are needed now in some form to eliminate the current trend of **Eternal Welfare**.

It's possible to "Game the System" right now, so that by posing as what you're not, you can live with a better income than you could ever earn on your own due to your lack of education, skills or initiative.

There are reports of boyfriend and girlfriend living together, hatching bastard kids and "Illegally" milking $70,000+ per year in legal welfare, housing, child care, food stamp and college subsidies from you and me. Food stamps are known in the **'milking welfare industry'** as **"Grub Stubs"**.

There are certainly **needy and deserving recipients** of all these different programs, but one of the most important requirements is that you be **absolutely "in-need"**. A favorite trick is hatching kids just to get subsidies because you're a single parent. Why not pay for one kid only, and why not sterilize repeat offenders (male and female) and why not require every recipient to perform some work for the benefits, or a requirement to repay some percentage of them when working again — off the welfare dole.

"Roosevelt started the WPA (Works Projects Administration) in 1939. WPA was the largest and most ambitious American New Deal agency, hiring millions of unemployed people (mostly unskilled men) to carry out public works projects, including the construction of public buildings and roads. Almost every community in the United States had a new park, bridge or school constructed by the agency."[14]

A friend has a hunting camp in one of central Pennsylvania's lush, hilly State Forests where I was invited several times to be part of the after Thanksgiving traditional ritual of deer hunting with other flatlanders, wannabe citified Rednecks.

The two story cabin was typical — bunk beds for 12, and a giant pot-bellied stove. It was built in the 30's by Roosevelt's WPA workers, and I believe leased from the PA State Forest Division. Captain Dick's buddies from all over would show up and you were introduced to them as, Billie-Bob & Earl, Swoopy, Jesus, Ralph — this one's a Jew, this guy's a Communist — and then the drinking, heroics and politics were repeated and embellished endlessly for three days straight. What fun! Every once-in-awhile somebody'd go out and let off a "near miss" at a deer.

I remember back in the 1960's, attending a "Rent Party" at some girl's home in Coconut Grove, a sometimes affluent **Havana North** suburb of South Miami. The entrance fee was, "Bring your own booze and $3 dollars." The refrigerator had a red light in it; the place was packed — clouds of pot fumes — **a bathtub full of 50 pound bags of U.S. rice and beans.** There were many strange characters lurking — one passing business cards out, **"Paladin – Have Gun Will Travel."**

There were no "EBT" or green "Access" welfare ATM cards then, so you could buy chips, dip and a six pack like you can now. Welfare recipients had to go somewhere to get a government handout, which didn't include party supplies. Maybe we should go back to that method. Maybe we can get some welfare recipients to help build their half-way shelters and some others to babysit their bastards while doing it, and some others to give them some mandatory skills training, etc., etc., etc.. Maybe they should be automatically enlisted in a 21st Century version of FDR's WPA to earn a paycheck, just like every other working American.

Maybe judges should add a caveat to criminal sentencing like, "You don't get out even after your sentence is complete, unless you've earned a High School Diploma, a **Locked up GED** so to speak. You don't get out until you accomplish something positive toward your rehabilitation. When you do get out, you report the next day for a WPA job where you report every day, or you go back into the cooler."

WPA jobs are paid minimum wage, say $10 per hour with an annual COLA adjustment and deductions for taxes, medical care and retirement, just like all the other real Americans. They can stay on their WPA job forever, if they want. They can work toward a better future, but these WPA jobs are a beginning, from digging up potatoes on a farm, to working to build things as in the past. If you don't fulfill your WPA work requirement, or get kicked out of it, your welfare ends — go back to living in a refrigerator box under a bridge!

In this year's Baltimore riots, none of those "Other people" missed any work, because they weren't working. They were collecting welfare and loot. I really believe they would work if there was something to work on, and that's the key!

What could WPA employees work on?

Take every manual labor, or unskilled public job away from Federal entities. Each State might run its own version of WPA following Federal guidelines. Funding for Federal projects should be apportioned to the supplying State entities.

The States will supply Welfare recipients first, then other willing workers and thirdly, green-card immigrants to its projects.

An equally difficult conundrum is that Unions are a tradition started in America's Industrial Revolution. It began in the mid 1800's, lasting until the early 1960s. From then on that Industrial Revolution moved to Asia, leaving the Unions behind. What's left today has itself entrenched in bureaucratic government services.

The SEIU represents practically every Government employee from city and state level to all Federal Bureaucrats, and I believe teachers too. They latched onto something that was sure to remain — bureaucrats. Maybe we should outsource for Bureaucrats. They'll work without Unions, glad to have a job.

As an American Tradition, Unions can't be banned like they're trying to do to religious symbolism. They might disappear from lack of use, and then **maybe they could reinvent themselves so that they again become a useful, sought after force in America,** as opposed to just one of the main reasons all the jobs are now elsewhere.

Suppose Unions supply labor for entities willing to pay for services on a contracted basis. The workers would be employees of the Union. A builder, for instance, would sign a contract for roofers and the Union would supply its roofing employees, and deal with them. The builder pays the union when the job is finished, and has no roofers on his payroll.

Governments would do the same, having the Union supply all the benefits, not the Government entity. In effect the Paying entity pays for a finished product, while the union manages the personnel and all their benefits, rather than just representing them.

The Federal Government already pays many separate contractors to supply a commodity or service. I have a son who works for a contractor, providing a service to the Federal Government. There's no hassles for the Government. The Contractor doesn't get paid if they don't perform. Let the Union just be one more contractor for general services with a "No Strike" contract.

Why not have the new WPA build an American Wall, like the Great Wall of China, all 13,171 miles of it. [15] Circle our US mainland borders and add an "X" across the middle and do exactly what the Chinese did during the Ming Dynasty. They fortified it and added military garrisons at intervals here and there. Why not make it Homeland Security's troops' [16] new homes.

With some imagination and clever planning it could be a project where the rest of the world might wonder at its grandeur and remark also at its security curtain. **It could be a National start for the minds and hearts of any and all beginning, productive Americans — one of our 21st Century WPA projects, the main and enduring one**. Other WPA efforts can be initiated as needed to mitigate increasing Welfare Rolls and to foster a work ethic where needed.

WPA projects must be planned around the concept that **hand labor is more important than automation** is in this case. Rural and remote projects must also include WPA provided housing, such as FEMA trailers.

We live in an era of mind blowing, innovative technological advancement. This unfortunately eliminates many less skilled occupations. It also is helping to create longer welfare lines for those less skilled.

Here's a simple, actual example. Many cities now have trash trucks with an automated trashcan grabber that dumps your junk and garbage into the truck without the need for humans to attend to those tasks. This eliminates one or two jobs on each trash truck, where the now unemployed are probably on the welfare rolls, thanks to that automation.

Is this a misguided outlook by city fathers? Is it better to issue paychecks or welfare checks? I believe the phrase is, **"Let's start thinking outside the box."**

This issue is important to consider in the long term, because technology is rapidly replacing human jobs with robot jobs. How do we employ people when there are no jobs? Robotics usually replaces routine repetitive jobs now. As time goes on, artificial intelligence, virtual reality and nano technology will replace most every job, even those needing analysis and decision making. I guarantee somebody is working on robots to make love to you too. Once artificial intelligence takes over that risqué venture, we're completely useless — and lonely too! If they invent boy robots and girl robots, what then?

Google has cars running around, here and there, without you in control. How's it going to work when you want to dig out as the light changes? Navigating the I-495 beltway around DC is everybody going from zero to 90 every half mile — with you in your Google mobile losing ground every half mile. They have to test that concept by going around DC 10,000 times until it learns how to not come in last! In the meantime I want a car with my own gas pedal and horn!

DARPA[17] is adopting research into military weapons that have independent ideas of what to do next without long distance guidance — Google drones maybe — or Hal in charge!

Great thinkers should be brought together to analyze and divine its planned evolution — invent a responsible and ordered long range flexible plan! It might possibly prohibit automating certain classes of work purely to manage the needs of the unskilled, working their way off the dole — basically just a job, any job.

COMPLETE INDEPENDENCE

What Does The Word "Independence" Mean?

"Word Web Pro" states: "Freedom from control or influence of another or others"

California wanted to build a new San Francisco-to-Oakland bay bridge within sight of the Golden Gate Bridge. Who built it? A Chinese Construction firm with Chinese labor and Chinese steel.

Do you have a cell-phone, a computer, a flat-panel television? Most every version of these nice-to-have commodities is built in Oriental countries — not invented there, but produced there. Open up one of them and you'll be confronted with integrated circuit electronic **Chips**, the marvelous, modern miniaturization of electronics that has enabled the world to evolve at light speed since the discovery of the "Transistor Effect" by scientists at Bell Laboratories in 1947. You will also notice that a "Made in Korea, China, Japan or Taiwan" stamp is on most of them today.

Go to Wal-Mart or Home Depot and search for an American made screw-gun or screwdriver, TV table or dungarees?

Nothing Is Made Here Anymore!

There are obvious reasons for this of course, such as lower labor cost, even including the long distance shipping to get them here. The quality of their products is top shelf, and selections are modern and complete. Obviously Americans are not making these commodities. American manufacturing infrastructure to build these products is rusting and crumbling. As the lines at American payroll windows shrink, welfare lines expand. This is a sad commentary for American leadership. There are other aspects of all this — seldom considered!

Strategic Independence

Suppose the US gets into a rumble with the Chinese? Can you imagine this scenario? Every US Government entity has computers, millions of them, all full of Chinese chips. Do you wonder how they are hacking our secrets so easily?

Where would we get replacement parts? We'd have to place orders with Chinese factories to get more computers so we could go to war with them and blow up their factories, even the underground ones.

We could hire Chinese Border Guards for much less than we can supply our own US minted copies down along the Mexican border.

The new Chinese guards would come with their own Chinese uniforms and Made-in-China US flags. Since they're not unionized, we'd save enough to order more computers and cell-phones. Coincidently, I was hungry and just stopped to make a Chinese tuna fish sandwich. It was tasty.

What does all that mean? To me, the guy with an RV, camped in the desert with solar panels and a wind mill is truly independent — until he has to drive somewhere else.

What does Energy Independence mean to America? We always seem to get light when we flip a switch. We always get a TV picture. Although the price had gone up for gasoline in the past, we still managed to go someplace. Higher energy prices raised our cost-of-living, but we still managed. The $100 barrel of oil was employing many workers in that industry who are joining the unemployment rolls now when crude is $24 per barrel.

Saudi Arabia (OPEC) I believe is trying to initiate a "gas-war" offensive. Now that Iran is free to tap their vast oil reserves too, the prospects for US energy dominance is further eroding since the current administration has unlocked Iran's cash stash. American producers have recently laid off 25,000 oil-shale field workers. Oil needs to stay above $40 per barrel.

Quick cosmetic fixes are baloney. We shouldn't need to import gasoline, because we don't have enough of our own refining capacity. Build some more refineries — oops I forgot; the EPA won't let us.

Colonial fires of independence are what created this Nation. Why are we so dependent on the rest of the world now — is it out-of-balance trade agreements, environmentalists and/or unions? Is it somebody's Socialist master plan?

Today's global economy means we are dependent on other Nations for many of our needs. As long as we're satisfied with the availability, price and quality, no one complains much. But we don't control commerce outside our borders and therefore have various levels of satisfaction with it, and a lot of unemployment because of it.

Oriental electronics and automobiles are top shelf. Third world's clothes and shoes are in every closet. South American produce is as good as it gets. Foreign petroleum is in every car, and it works well.

In spite of the current government, we are beginning to exploit our own energy potential whether they like it or not. It'll be interesting to see how environmentalist and Progressive legislators try to marginalize that effort.

I belong to the American Legion and our local Honor Guard, which provides services to mark military tribute for veterans affairs, memorials, etc. — wearing my uniform, with its Made-in-China shirt!

There are kinks in this arrangement. We have no control over these purveyors of products we can't do without??? Free Trade agreements have eliminated taxing as a tool or economic weapon. We don't have free trade agreements with the oil cartels (OPEC) who fluctuate the price of their product on the whim of a few bankers, oil potentates and Mullahs, and who vote against us in 75% of UN issues.

Energy

We should develop US oil resources "full speed ahead", and at the same time, exploit all other energy sources (nuclear – wind – CNG – natural gas - shale oil – coal – solar - bio-fuels and hydro), none needing to be invented and most are readily available today.

US energy infrastructure needs modernization and added capacity. Finish the Keystone pipe. **It only adds 800 miles of pipe to the 1,382,570 miles of it already buried in or running over US soil.** Add new refineries and LNG (liquid natural gas) facilities to aid in exporting our vast natural gas supplies. These steps are considered short term — five years.

The 2016 budget bill, while not at all what the right-leaning electorate wanted, did eliminate some restrictions on exporting US energy, and may well mitigate the current slump in energy jobs.

Long term, a concerted all-out USA technological blitz should be to the development of an all new energy source, akin to JFK's "Man on the Moon in Ten Years" challenge/goal. When accomplished, America can be the world's largest exporter of energy. Let Vladimir and OPEC plant potatoes.

We are well on the way toward that goal with current efforts in hydrogen fuel-cell and Lithium-ion battery technology. There seems to be no better long range solution right now to get you back and forth to the grocery store or work. The fuel is hydrogen, the simplest and lightest and most abundant element in the universe (Atomic #1). There are no downsides to this solution, including the lack of pollutants — just that nasty old water dripping from the tailpipe.

The goal here seems to be, "how do we make the solution affordable enough to park in your garage, how to develop the infrastructure to support it, and **what to do for the industries supplanted by it.** Ten years ought to do it.

Further down the road is energy derived from methyl hydrate, otherwise known as deep sea ice that burns. Then of course, there's the nuclear energy source we pioneered development of after we flattened parts of Japan with it in 1945. Newer nuclear power generation technology is safer, but still costly to build and maintain.

Why the hell are we still using coal-fired electric generation? Export all the coal to the third world and/or subsidize scrubbers for existing smokestack emissions to keep coal fired power generation and mining industries viable until that natural resource is exhausted.

Blessed with many and abundant natural energy resources, we should continue to explore, expand and exploit. We have the capacity, skills and the need to expand and control these commodities worldwide and to lead development of the next centuries' energy.

We must keep meat and potatoes on dinner tables by continuing existing industries until we run out of whatever natural resource they're using up. We are in the cat-bird seat right now and are able to control the worldwide energy infrastructure well into the future.

Manufacturing

As you drive by another era's manufacturing ghost towns, such as Bethlehem or Pittsburg, Pennsylvania, Youngstown, Ohio — the vast windowless manufacturing ghettos in other once great Rust Belt cities like Detroit, what do you think of? "Isn't that a great place to put another useless mall? Where do all those people work now? Why are all those local stores boarded up?"

Anybody know why or who did it? Unions? Union work rules? Overzealous, elitist, conniving, "Nobody would piss on them if they were on fire" Government Regulators?

A widget maker in this business climate has to stay competitive so that you'll buy his widgets. Go to your nearest Home Depot, to the tools department and price a Milwaukee screw-gun and a comparable Rigid or Makita version. The made-in-the-USA Milwaukee tool cost $200+, while the Rigid lists at $79. Everyone but the contractor will buy the $79 tool made in China or Japan. The contractor buys because of name recognition maybe, but guess what, the $79 Rigid works great and you can buy three for the Milwaukee price. But now, some Milwaukee tools come from Milwaukee, China too.

How about this American workers? The 2017 Buick Envision van is built in China and available this summer!

The American manufacturer is being priced out of the market by out-sourcing and because he has to pay for counter-productive work rules, escalated wages and benefits.

For those who don't know, "Union Work Rules" basically govern who can do what, where and when in union controlled shops. I was witness to an example of this, at "Philco-Ford" in the mid-70s. Few millenials recognize the Philco name these days. It disappeared into a typical outsourced, union-caused vanishing act.

In the mid 70's I managed a force of computer technicians who fixed a warehouse full of Burroughs, room-filling computer mainframes for Philco-Ford.

We were given an office/workshop area at their "C-Street" Philadelphia manufacturing plant where they had some of these computers. Philco supplied two dismantled workbenches for us — each had six screw-in pipe legs.

The union "Movers" brought the bench tops, but they wouldn't screw the legs in! We had to wait until later in the day for union "Millwrights" whose job it was to do such important tasks. Me and a colleague screwed them all in and stood them up, a two minute task.

We caught hell too, because it wasn't our job to do. Hence, the Union Work Rules forced Philco-Ford to employ people who were not needed, only to do a minor, insignificant task.

Therefore Philco's products had to include salaries, expenses and benefits for those two "Millwrights" which they probably didn't really need — the union said they did, "Or else"?

The pendulum had swung in the 70's, way too far, causing things like "Outsourcing". I'll bet, that when I drive to visit my kids in Philadelphia the next time, that the old "Philco-Ford" plant on "C" street is windowless now as well — at best, maybe a warehouse with only six employees.

The well known quality furniture manufacturer "Ethan Allen" in Bradford, PA was closed as was the "Olean Tile Co." in close by Olean New York — companies who couldn't compete anymore I guess.

Don't get me wrong. Unions still have some benefit today. They generally keep tight control of their members, knowing that their days are numbered I suppose.

Union apprenticeship programs are still a great idea and usually turn out well qualified journeymen workers. A union trained electrician for instance always knows all the building code rules and time-tested techniques that "jack-of-all tradesmen" won't — or will ignore.

I had a young friend living in the Florida Panhandle, who was planning to move back to his Chicago hometown, so he could get a union roofers' job at $40 an hour ($83,200 per year). I don't begrudge him the exorbitant imbalanced wage, but how does roofing compare to a teacher's wage ($44,500 — K to 12)?

No wonder there are hordes of skilled Mexican roofers jumping the border fences to cash in, and get Obama benefits to boot!

I believe Union hierarchy is stuck in a time warp. No enterprise survives in today's technological whirlwind without loads of forward thinking. They need to reinvent themselves into something business wants instead of something business wants to kick out.

Maybe they could evolve into a business where they manage the costs to produce a service for a price per man-hour and survive only if they are competitive, not because they have nasty enforcers. If they don't modernize and shape up, they'll evaporate into memories, just like manual typewriters and carbon paper.

The problem is, how do we maintain the quality of American workmanship and products without the enormous difference in labor costs to produce them? We need new ideas here — soon!

"Made In USA"

We need a concerted effort to "Buy American". Every hard-goods for sale has a "Country of Origin" stamped on it somewhere. That's different for some fresh food, but I believe there's a move afoot to require that labeling too.

I'd like to see all purveyors make American items more prominent in store displays. All catalogs should list "Country of Origin" in every advertisement. Retailers should prominently and proudly display that American Made fact. I'll bet that the retail industry will be pleasantly surprised at the result. Shoppers today, trying to save a buck in this inflationary economy, including me, automatically assume that foreign commodities today are always less expensive than those crafted or grown here. More and more that isn't the case. While shopping, check commodities with manufacturer names you don't recognize, because many major producers are outsourced and higher priced. I think they are beginning to take advantage of the notion that "foreign goods are always cheaper". Not always!

Not too many years ago I believe the Federal Government had required "Made in America" on all purchases. I remember back in the 1970s, the company I was working for at the time (Burroughs Corp.), was preparing a bid on some computer equipment for the State of New Jersey. The bid had a requirement to "Buy American", but there was a caveat that "elsewhere" was OK if there was no other source, but had to have 95% "American Made"[18] contents. In this case, I had to open up one of these computer systems and actually count all the computer chips not made in the U.S. to see if the 95% quota was met — **back in the 70's.** I'll take bets that one manufactured today would be reversed — 5% US and 95% from Oriental climes.

I realize that Free Trade Agreements changed the whole dynamic for the US and now we're having a hard time competing. Ruinous Union contracts along with global trade rules put us way behind the 8-ball.

When those trade agreements were signed, union agreements should've been unsigned. All of the points I've mentioned in preceding pages should have been realized before giving the business away to the rest of the world.

As I was editing the copy for this book, sitting on my sons front porch in the tiny farm town of Shinglehouse, PA, a nice, new, shiny red Kubota (Japanese) tractor drove down the street.

Agriculture

Farming and its American way-of-life has declined in this last century to a factory-farm, bio-engineered big business today. There's no doubt that there are economies of scale to be gained from this approach. It works very well and makes farm acreage more productive as a result, helping to compete with South American produce. But, something **"American"** is missing, dying or maybe already dead.

Drive through once lush and vital farmland, where most farms were fifty to two hundred acres, and what do you see today? You see abandoned, fallow fields awaiting a condo or mall developer. Nobody is there anymore. Should this way of life disappear in the name of progress? Should Mom & Pop grocery stores disappear in favor of a brand new mall with Wal-Mart and Home Depot eliminating 50 little stores in our once great little American towns — now boarding up?

I went into Meadville, Pennsylvania a few years ago to have lunch. It's a typical northwestern PA small to medium size country farm town, where well known and respected manufacturing of "Channel-Lock" hand tools takes place. You can buy a serviceable clone in Home-Depot, a mile down the road, for ⅓ the price. At 2 p.m. after the lunch hour, almost every storefront in Meadville is locked up tight. Store owners go home because everybody shops at Wal-Mart and Home Depot now.

Why not create Small-Town co-ops that receive tax breaks for start-ups, like New York is doing to attract new business — but in this case to keep business afloat, to revitalize the "downtown" way-of-life also.

Eliminate all tax breaks and loopholes for the Wal-Mart's of the world who hawk products not made by American Moms & Pops?

City and town planners must some way encourage downtown revitalization that keeps all the good restaurants, movie theatres and entertainment right next to whatever makes each little city unique. Encourage, with enticements, the VFW and American Legions to locate right in the middle of town.

In the little city of Olean, the "Lower Tier" of northwestern New York, a landmark right in the main intersection downtown, is a vacant seven or eight story old bank building. It's not only contributing to a decaying downtown, but looks like hell. I bet that was a vibrant corner, with successful shops and restaurants when it was full of bankers and secretaries. But now the main intersection is looking rundown.

I'm sure the town fathers have muddled over this issue more than once. Maybe some out-of-the-box thinking is needed there too.

If the city would donate that building to a nearby university with the caveat that they develop a new curriculum there of "City and Urban planning", that little downtown would be instantly revitalized and preserved.

I hate to say this, but the internet not only has immensely changed the whole world, but has also helped destroy "downtowns" by giving unfair advantage to on-line entrepreneurs who can offer products at less than your downtown hardware store can, simply because you don't have to pay sales tax.

I always use on-line sources because I can usually do it cheaper. I save the Pennsylvania six percent sales tax, because

I buy everything I can on-line and watch for the "free shipping" specials. The downtown store owner goes home after lunch.

Somehow, everything that made America good and great has been replaced in the name of progress, and toward Socialism. I believe we give subsidies to farmers, encouraging what I call Farm Welfare. Why not eliminate farm subsidies, except for **Organic Farm Co-Ops**, where farm acreage is limited to 200 acres in one-family farms.

Have you tasted a really delicious tomato in recent years? Genetic meddling has created a hardier, disease resistant red thing that looks like a great tomato — but it isn't! The skin is so tough you need a razor to cut it, and once you do, you have to take a second look to see what it is because you can't tell by tasting it.

I remember years ago, with my city folks, going over the bridge just to get a basket of South Jersey Marglobe tomatoes. I don't remember having tasted anything as good in years — a bacon, tomato and lettuce sandwich with mayo on white toast used to make me drool waiting for it.

You can still get good, tasty Marglobes today, but you still have drive to Jersey to get 'em. No seed purveyor has tinkered with their genes.

As you wander through the produce department in your local supermarket you see "Organic" selections of most veggies, but they cost more. Why? To peddle Organic veggies, meat and dairy, a farmer's product has to be Government Certified that it met the requirements, such as:[19]

- No chemicals = more labor. Pesticides kill weeds, while hand labor is required for organic certification.

- Demand overwhelms supply. Prices are higher.

- Organic farmland represents only **.09%** of available worldwide farmland.

- Higher cost of fertilizer for organic crops.

- Sewage sludge and chemicals are cheaper than compost and animal manure.

- Crop rotation — Organic farmers rotate crops to keep their soil healthy, preventing weed growth. After harvesting, organic farmers usually grow "cover crops," next which adds nitrogen to the soil.

- Conventional farmers may elect to grow a profitable crop instead.

- Post harvesting handling costs.

- To avoid cross-contamination, organic produce must be separated from conventional produce after being harvested.

- Organic Certification costs?

- Strict daily record-keeping must be available for inspection.

- Organic farms must pay an annual inspection & certification fee.

- Costs for covering higher loss rate — Insurance.

- Synthetic pesticides repel insects and antibiotics maintain the health of the livestock — not allowed in Organic farming.

- Organic foods face a shorter storage time and shelf life.

- Better living conditions for livestock.

- Organic livestock feed can cost twice as much as conventional.

- Organic food grows more slowly.

- The organic farmer refrains from using chemicals and growth hormones.

Subsidies.

In '08, spending on farm subsidies was $7.5 billion while **only $15 million for organic**.

In the mid 80's, New Zealand eliminated farm subsidies despite initial wrangling and today its farming GDP is a respectable 5%. Its "Farmer" way-of-life is once again respected and productive without government intrusion and control.

I travel a lot, and this story almost makes me cry. A favorite movie of mine is called, "Doc Hollywood". It's not Academy Award material for the Tinsel Town crowd, but for me it is, because good old America is so well represented in its satire.

Its melodrama represents what once was America. "Grady" is what we should be subsidizing. It's the heart of America, with **active and producing** farms shutting down — and with rusty tractors lying around and barns caving in. The farmers' kids are signing up for welfare.

Let the UN manage somebody else — not us!

Is our Green Government encouraging & coercing urban immigration where we can be easily controlled — leaving a vast "Department of the Interior, Bureau of Land Management, EPA'd, **American Outback**"?

Sometime in the near future we'll have to get a passport to drive through it. **UNESCO** (a UN Group) now controls our Yellowstone National Park where Old Faithful is, prohibiting development **outside** its boundaries.

Joe Baylis' gold mine was outside the boundaries of Yellowstone National Park. It fulfilled all state and federal environmental requirements. But those facts didn't stop UNESCO from exercising its authority over Baylis' land. According to the World Heritage treaty, UN jurisdiction now also includes "critical buffer zones." So when World Heritage Committee members from Europe and Asia appeared in Wyoming in 1995 to help radical environmentalist fight the environmentally friendly mining company, they claimed and won the right to censure human activity within that entire ecosystem. In other words, "systems thinking" rather than scientific facts and logic had prevailed. Does Baylis still own whatever gold may be there if mined, or had the UN just swiped it?

What would be the boundaries of the Yellowstone World Heritage ecosystem? They are not yet established, but would include parts of "Utah, Idaho, Wyoming and Montana, an area of between 14 and 18 million acres." Yellowstone Park itself covers only about 2.2 million acres. Must the United States then submit to UN regulations for human activity within this entire region, or any US region for that matter?

They arbitrarily increased the park's size from 2.2 million acres to over a 14 million acre **"critical buffer zone".** You got it right — the UN told the US how to manage its own resources.

We should throw the whole bunch in the East River and knock the building down on top of them to make sure they stay there.[20] Didn't the Obama administration just go behind our backs to get the UN to add some caveats to help convince Iran's Mullahs to sign the US Nuclear Treaty so Kerry and Obama wouldn't have to mention what they are and include them in the US Treaty? The UN Gruberized the treaty for us!

An overzealous political administration can jam through UN treaties to govern things here that might be incompatible with the next political bunch, or with US citizens in general. To help mitigate that, maybe all treaties should be approved only by a two thirds majority **(Supermajority)** of both Houses of Congress — no exceptions.

<u>Strategic</u> Independence

What does that mean? As stated earlier, we'd have to order spare parts from China before we went to war with them. That's a ridiculous thought isn't it? But, we don't have much of a steel industry left. The Chinese have built a bridge for us recently. Fortunately we have more than enough fuel for any endeavor, despite OPEC, Vladimir or Khomeini.

We must be able to produce strategic supplies for whatever military or security endeavor we attempt without having to import even one nut or bolt, chip — or Russian rocket engine! We must design and build every ship, plane, satellite or space ship here, with American brainpower, manpower and US commodities. We shouldn't have to rent space or a seat on a Soviet or Chinese rocket to get to the next galaxy.

In eliminating our dependence on foreign supply lines we can tell them all to go to hell and put Americans back to work at the same time. Other commodities can be imported, but not those required for **complete strategic independence**.

These Strategic Industries might only be staffed with American citizens using American computers, tools and working over secure American only networks.

There can be **no diversity** in this strategic scheme.

MILITARY & SPACE SUPERIORITY

The title of this section covers many topics that, of necessity or maybe self preservation, should get only a broad brush here. But, one of the overall points to be discussed is this.

I believe most Americans are tired of the constant involvement in trying to mother-hen the whole world. I believe most of us would rather it evolves or perishes without our meddling. Let NATO and the UN meddle.

To that end I believe that we should protect ourselves with an **impregnable** "Star Wars" shield, as was first envisioned by Ronald Regan, and to protect **all** of our borders as well, with fortress-like security.

If our interests are attacked anywhere else in the world, an immediate and total devastation of the perpetrator is necessary. There's no such thing as a proportional response.

That'd be hard to accomplish however, with the nature of today's "Terrorist" approach to warfare. The lesson to be dealt to our enemies is, "Stay home or face annihilation" — or at the very least, destruction of their home country back to the Stone Ages.

By that I mean eliminate every semblance of modernity. Destroy all power generation, all bridges, all port, air and rail facilities, all military and police facilities, all communication, internet apparatus and related facilities, all transportation and major highways, making them one big pothole. Send their satellites out towards Mars.

BUT — ISIS is already living in a Middle East pothole. They must be kept marginalized for at least two generations while the Muslim religion tries to erase malevolent thought from their offspring's minds — by not teaching them old Fundamental Sharia precepts in the Madrasas (schools).

The nature of today's conflict is like fighting a religious cancer that's metastasized, eating at the whole planet. That usually means in medical terms, that you are losing the battle and it's time to put your affairs in order.

Paris and Brussels today is once again under siege, not by Nazis like 71 years ago, but by an ancient malevolence using ancient fundamentalist parables as today's gospel plus modern bomb vests, grenades and Kalashnikov's.

This all suggests we cannot deal with their modern religious pestilence by trying to win using conventional warfare, or by negotiating a joke, like we just did with Iran. Never trust a rug merchant. We must reinforce the notion **"Don't Tread On Me"**, which by the way goes both ways!

We've amply demonstrated the folly of trying to separate warring ideologies and teaching them Democracy. We stopped at the 37th parallel in North Korea and 60 years later we're still camped there and the Kim regime now has nukes and missiles of its own, a much more devastating threat now — just what Iran wants to be. What's stopping North Korea? Is it because the US Military is camped on their doorstep. Would Iran and ISIS be much of a threat today if the US was permanently camped in Iraq? Thanks again Barak.

Would Putin be taking over Syria today if we had been there as Obama boasted when he drew al-Assad's red line? There' was a jackass on both ends of that line.

Just to show his barbarity, "Little Kim" now executes his "nay-Sayers" by shooting them with his personal artillery cannon. A little bullet isn't sufficient for him. He needs a whole cannon ball to do in the fool who fell asleep while he was pontificating.

We should have continued across the 37th parallel and kicked his old man's ass all the way out — back in 1954 when I signed up to do just that. He must have been scared when he got wind of me coming because he signed a Peace Treaty only 94 days later.

We haven't finished the job there, have we? We should quit trying to be a mediator and only go to battle as the **total conqueror** — just as we did in Germany and Japan.

Basically, we flattened Germany, then fire-bombed it just to make sure. We firebombed Japan first and then nuked them twice. We rebuilt their governments, helped keep Germany fed during the Berlin Airlift and look at what we have there now — one of Europe's most stable, and friendly governments. Japan is now a staunch ally. We have permanent bases there, in Guam and also maintain a major military presence in Rheine-Mein, probably forever. We had the same accommodation in Iraq, but our current administration said "No. We don't need to keep troops there. We need the money for "free shit and phones!"

I believe it's a horrible mistake relinquishing all military bases because a war is over. America paid dearly with her mangled soldier's limbs and lives to help or conquer somebody.

A permanent bastion at least, should be part of the price for their sacrifice.

The U.S. has Puerto Rico, Guam and Guantanamo Bay since the Spanish American war in 1898 and now has a perpetual lease from Cuba for Gitmo. Keeping that lease falls under the same rubric. I'll bet Raúl Castro wants it back and I'll bet Obama will try to convince us to make peace by giving it back — **to hell with that!** I'll bet he's pushing that request just to keep his campaign promise, "Close Guantanamo". Close the stockade maybe, but never give Guantanamo Bay Naval base back. America's blood has paid for it!

Castro is claiming reparations must be given for a trade embargo enforced there since 1960 or so. What Obama seems to be ignoring is the cost for all the US business interest seized by the Castro regime, valued today around seven billion.

The expatriate Cubans, now American citizens, have additional gripes. When they escaped Castro's Communism, they lost everything. Those that had some money hid it in the walls of their homes there to no avail. Those business people who fled lost whatever they created.

I lived in Miami in 1959 and had a next door neighbor who left behind a Coca Cola bottling company and a Volkswagen Dealership. Today's South Florida Americans are still penalized by Castro when they send money to relatives left behind. The Castro's keep half of it for themselves!

There are a lot of those American refugee-citizens and their first generation offspring that would tell Obama to do nothing more there for the time being and to give both of the Castro brothers time to die in hopes a more agreeable regime replaces them.

I bet, given time with no more than trade between us, that they will become a welcomed neighbor with Guantanamo as a symbol of national unity.

Guantanamo's perpetual lease was willingly given to the US after the Spanish American war in appreciation for America's Monroe Doctrine, [21] forcing Spain to relinquish control of Cuba, therefore allowing it to become a sovereign nation.

We "Advised" in Vietnam and by bombing Hanoi, had that "conflict" won at one time. The Peaceniks were running that advisory operation, so we stopped and basically got kicked out of "Nam", just as the French did before we showed up. What arrogance we had! What did we accomplish with 58,000 lives there and 120 billion dollars?

In the case of Muslim terrorists (ISIS — al-Qaida — Boko Haram — Hamas) by whatever name they call themselves, they are a fifth century aberration of the old Fundamentalist book of the Muslim faith.

Once started, it's going to take generations to teach new young Muslim students in the Madrasas, that they have been listening to and learning from ancient parables (stories) that desperately need modern interpretation. They are using modern military technology and modern social media to prosecute a terror war based on **ancient Fundamental beliefs**.

Those beliefs weren't just Muslim, but Christian and Jew as well. The difference is that the Christians and Jews have modernized their beliefs while some Muslims have not. The Crusade is against us this time

Until that realization takes hold we must prepare for a protracted intelligence and ideologic battle. Modern thinking

Muslims must **lead** that battle — in their homelands, **<u>not here and not us anymore</u>**! Our Washington DC jackass gave up our ace in that hellhole!

The Kurds, Jordanians, Saudi Arabia, Turkey and even Iran are beginning to do their share of cleaning up the mess in their part of the world, and we must do our part in helping them. **But what help do we provide?**

Joe Biden was right long ago when he said we should encourage Iraq to split up into three nations, the Kurds, Sunni and Shia, and it's probably still good advice. The only major pitfall in that effort is how to get them to share their oil revenues, because large parts of Iraq have no oil. The border areas with Iran and Kuwait have some of the largest reserves in the world.

It's well documented that all of the conflict engulfing the Middle East is involved in one way or another with its rich reserves of crude oil. Iran and Russia are jockying for that prize right now! ISIS is funded by it.

The US, UK, France, Russia, et al, have at the highest Government and Corporate levels, plundered and gerrymandered sovereign lands for what's under them.[22]

Just as Socialism is waging a war for the compliant minds of the many traditionally uninformed and the new American Millennial voters, so have the "K" street Oil and Gas lobbyist in Washington.

All the world's shadow governments have been manipulating both sides of every conflict to get their pieces of the Middle East's oil and its revenues. It's a good thing that wine isn't the coveted commodity, because we'd be droning Italy and Northern California right now and launching cruise missiles at somebody here. Technology will eventually supplant the need for **"Black Gold"**. What then??

Does anyone really think Americans gives a damn about the Middle East? We went to war there to guarantee you could continue to get a full gas tank at your nearby convenience store for under three dollars a gallon, nothing more.

But now the game is changing. All of a sudden new drilling techniques have opened up huge reserves here in the USA, which means to this neocon that we don't need their oil, "cause we got our own".

In fact, if we wanted we could easily supply those who want our natural gas and many other nations as well. LNG (**Liquid** **Natural Gas**) is the answer to shipping gas across the oceans. All we have to do is increase our LNG refining capacity (converting gas to liquid) which has been stalled by our Nanny Government politics.

The "Environment" is this Government's ploy to elicit help from voters on the Socialist Left, to stall oil and gas development until our own "Shadow Government" feels the time is right.

Most Americans are wondering why the Obama regime is trying to ignore calls for help from the Middle East. The answer is simple. "We don't need their damned oil no more!"

"Let 'em plant potatoes." Let's keep the exporting of our natural resources at full capacity while developing alternate technology for that day when we start to run out.

We've been brainwashed by lobbyist for the Energy and War Industries, and by the "Fat Cat" oligarchy[23] that really decides what's next. We have few choices. We can recognize the "Fat Cats" as a new wing of government who have us all go to war anywhere they want to reap the gold — or find a way to control those who govern us behind our backs. Wasn't Prescott Bush thrown out of the US Senate for doing something like that?[24]

The Culture of Jihad

In the meantime, we might consider preventing anyone who fits the ISIS mold from entering the US, and any American who attempts radicalization elsewhere from ever returning here. They can stay there and go get a job in the oil industries sprouting up elsewhere.

Past American immigration laws (pre 1965) had quotas that forbade certain classes of immigrants and **refugees**. We need that now. Did we not try to ban visitors and émigrés from African Countries last year when Ebola was out of control? Once that plague was contained, there was no more talk of denying visas back and forth to Liberia, Sierra Leone and Guinea.

I propose that we only reopen that avenue to Sunni and Shia Muslims only if their disease is cured — until they get their religious beliefs under control — several hundred years maybe!

Militant Islam today is a demented cult that refuses to accept the right to believe as you wish. You must believe as they do and submit to Allah's dictates or it's a "Jihad" on you. It is just like Hitler's "Final Solution" to purify the Arian race by eliminating Jews.

ISIS, in the name of Muhammad, is on the march to eliminate not only Jews and Christians, **but any Muslim that doesn't follow Sharia law too.** They'll probably start chopping up Mormons and the Amish after they run out of Christians and Jews, and then Quakers, Vikings and Zulu's — maybe those few who live on the Falkland Islands. They gotta' go too!

I'm sure our CIA and military intelligence agencies are well aware exactly where we should carpet bomb, and I suspect that should be ISIS headquarters in Syria.

I believe we must increase and reinforce our clandestine agencies up to a wartime footing, supplemented by their management of Seal Teams, Army Rangers and Air Force drones.

Further "Boots-on-the-ground forces in the Middle East must by **indigenous** soldiers. The strength of our undercover warrior forces should be increased as a matter of **permanent, on-going national security.**

The Geneva Convention only refers to **uniformed** soldiers, which ISIS are not. I believe, after they've been water boarded, the next step is to pull out their fingernails and toenails one at a time. If that doesn't loosen them up, drill holes in all their teeth — as a start!

Ronald Regan wasn't successful in his attempt to institute his SDI ("Star Wars") coverage over the homeland. But the threat of it helped convince our Cold War adversaries we were serious. But guess what? **We are in need of that actual deterrent now**.

Putin is starting to push around his former USSR associates — China is flashing around their new copies of stolen US military technology and various despots are juggling their A-bombs and long range missiles.

During all previous wars we were protected by two huge oceans. Now we're only hours away from today's Armageddon[25] weapons, most of which are aimed at us.

Although shelved then, there's been continued progress in that Star Wars arena. The US has been experimenting and developing technologies to protect us and obliterate adversaries ever since. There are many approaches, some now operational, but not at the level to assure that American security and technology reigns supreme.

We've abrogated our control of the near space arena **and must retake it.**

I don't believe we've been putting unarmed satellites up there all this time. The question is, are they defensive, offensive or both? I sure hope **both** is the answer.

Somehow, some of our adversaries' satellites have to be executed to send a message. **"We own near space. Be careful".**

Maybe we should scramble all Iranian and Syrian communication satellites and have our submarines dig up Internet connections to the Middle East, just to lessen Twitter and Facebook terrorist' recruiting?

We're in the beginning of an Internet and "Near Space" standoff and must send a clear message to the rest of the world — "We created and own those frontiers. Play by our rules or else." Let's have a demonstration of those principles after dark on the next July 4[th.]

ENTITLEMENTS

Birth To Death

Any time "Entitlements" are mentioned, politicians begin to cringe at the thought that their name might be attached to something negative regarding the treasured lifelines Americans have paid into. Just because many of us are over 65 doesn't mean we can't shoot straight anymore.

Anyone whose worked has paid into Social Security and Workers' Comp, yet the Pols are afraid to touch it or try to improve it in any way, because they don't know how to sell it to people who've lived a long time and are expecting it to be there when they retire.

Give them a good long range plan that addresses all the foreseen contingencies and you probably can sell any good idea.

The current ACA, "Obama Care" jammed down our throats, "Gruberized" so we couldn't fathom what's in it, started from the well-intended proposition that **"Everybody needs medical care"**.

It's hard to argue against that viewpoint. It's easy to poke holes in its implementation and the gerrymandering of options, rules, implementation and, "If you like your doctor, you can keep your doctor," bullcrap. Still, the basic aim is worthwhile.

Their laughable approach to its implementation continues to reinforce the Reganism, "The most terrifying words in the English language are: **"I'm from the government and I'm here to help."**

ACA has survived all the Supreme Court challenges so far and will probably be the first fight in the next Congress. Learning from the Obama Care Cluster-F%#&, should introduce the dumbest of them to the notion that the **KISS Principal**[26] should have been followed.

In absorbing all the criticism tossed his way, President Obama keeps challenging Congress to come up with a better plan. To date none has surfaced. Well, guess what. I have one, and it adheres to the KISS principal — satisfies the dictum, "Everybody needs medical care" and it **will** cost everyone something, <u>because it is an **Entitlement**</u>.

A Plan To Cover Everybody

A — People who have no insurance

Can't afford it

Don't give a damn

Young — will live forever

B — People who had an Insurance Work Benefit

Medical savings benefit

Family plan

Minimal coverage with deductable co-pay

Cadillac plan

C — People who paid for their own insurance

Medical savings benefit

Family plan

Minimal coverage with deductible co-pay

Cadillac plan

D — ACA Victims

Everybody today

Before ACA (Obamacare - D), "B" and "C" didn't worry much about "A" because if "A" was in trouble, there was always the hospital emergency room.

The hospital usually provided immediate care, but seldom got paid for its effort and some of them consequently have eliminated any emergency room care — closed it down! This placed an unsustainable load on other hospitals and it was barely adequate for those "A" people who had no other choice.

The previous healthcare system left a lot to be desired for the "A" people, but everybody else got along somehow on their current arrangements. Everyone was taken care of under that system, but it definitely needed improving in many areas. This current bureaucratic joke, Obamacare, aptly demonstrates also, that business should be left to the business world.

Typically, there are always caring people who feel the need to make things better — they mostly seem to vote Left, while the self sufficient were reasonably happy following the tried and true principals that got them into their more secure world. They pay more attention to their own progress because they feel that most of the rest of society can make it too if they want to work for it.

There's lack of foresight in both arenas. Consider if you will, that "B" and "C" were pretty much satisfied, while only "A" needed some kind of help. The Left needs to continue helping the downtrodden and mother-hen everybody — so how do you correct that without rearranging everybody else's ordered life in the process, like Obamacare did?

Family Doctor?

In the past, most American's had a "Family Doctor" where, even if you couldn't pay, you got most things taken care of — up to casts for broken bones and at-home maternity services. "Take two of these and call me in the morning".

Doc would give you some narcotic to ease your suffering, and tell you to go to bed. He'd recommend available Government-provided home respite care. He'd give you a specialist referral just like he had for your ancestors.

If he thought you had a tumor, he'd give you a referral. If you couldn't afford the referral, he gave you some narcotic to ease your suffering and told you to go to bed — where you also usually died.

Life was much simpler then. The nuts were locked up in an asylum somewhere and most people had some health care provided. Most family doctors would take care of anybody who walked in the door. The better off had better choices, but everybody had someone looking out for their health.

Why not subsidize and augment the existing cadre of America's Family Doctors by paying for <u>every</u> American's **"Family Doctor" level of care**? Every American has a family doctor this way. Basic medical services, like shots for kids, all your generic meds and basic geriatric medical supplies are provided. Every Family Doctor, nationwide, has access to your medical history and treatment, every pharmacy can see your prescription history, and fill your generic prescriptions.

If your doctor refers you to a specialist or a hospital for an operation, you must have private insurance or cash to cover it

— no exceptions. Otherwise, he'll medicate you to make you comfortable up to the end — **as had always been done?**

Nurse practitioners can help fill the gap when a house call is needed. These government subsidized Family Doctor businesses can also serve as intern proving grounds for future MDs. Urban ghettos can be served by Federal Clinics offering the same services and care — no more, no less.

Insurance benefits, **without government oversight,** for care beyond what your Primary Physician, your family doctor provides, can more readily be offered by your employer now, and Insurance companies stay in business. The left and the Nanny Government can feel enlightened and that they have somehow fulfilled their need to nurture and govern something.

If you don't like the free "Family Doctor" care being provided, you can always pay cash or for private insurance that would cater to the more affluent for elitist services provided by medical practitioners who might want to expand their horizons — and wallets.

The selection of services provided by these Family Doctor businesses should be created by the practitioners in that profession and include fair wages for their efforts. Basic dental and eye care could be included — nothing cosmetic, no false teeth and just one pair of basic goggles every five years.

How do we pay for all that?

Consider making Family Doctor Medical Care an entitlement just like Social Security, where everyone pays via a payroll deduction from wages earned. That's basically how Social Security is paid-for isn't it?

Payroll deductions would also even come now from welfare benefits, Medicaid, Social Security and Unemployment Compo. Make both of those "Trust Funds" inviolable, and control both contributions and payouts with an annual COLA adjustment.

A national database of health history can be set up for all Americans. It must be instantly available to all providers, so that your Primary Doctor's notes, recommendations and prescription history are available to every physician and pharmacy you might have to visit if you are away from your hometown.

If you're in Ethiopia, visit the local US Embassy. Your information will be available on-line there as well for the local witch-doctor. Press F8 for translation to Ethiopian. **KISS**.

How do you keep personal information from hackers or the NSA? When every baby is born, an RFID chip is implanted. When you visit your primary saw-bones, the chip, a thumb-print and a retina scan identifies you and you only.

If necessary, you may have to answer "What was your mother's maiden name?" too — once in a while! In a few generations, everybody will be in one gigantic hard drive (cloud).

Again, I believe it's called the **KISS** principal, **"Keep It Simple Stupid"**.

Social Security & Medicare

These are the major lifesavers of the American Dream — a grownup lifetime of dedicated work-everyday slavery, all aimed toward that day, waaaaaaay off in the future, when the Retirement Party is for you this time. That's one of the major reasons people show up every day, that long look toward the reward for chasing that dream.

I always worked and had enough cash to raise four kids, take vacations and generally lived the "good" life. My life or family, by no means, is an example of the "TV's Hendersons", but we're all typical, I suppose — could've done better. They're all grown up with their own families and tribulations, but for me now, "Thank God for Social Security".

Social Security paid out in 2012 over $140 billion, while taking in only $103 billion. Legislators are afraid to tackle the funding issues because they are liking their cushy jobs. But, something has to be done to maintain the current payout.

The obvious solution is to raise the retirement age every ten years to match the current escalated longevity estimates, and also adjust the annual taxpayer contributions by the COLA amount on <u>unlimited</u> earnings.

From 1989 to 2009, the Social Security Trust Fund was solvent. Since then it's had to secure Government Bonds. Actuarial estimates to the tune of 15 trillion dollars are necessary to preserve solvency (an Unfunded Liability). We're having a hard time paying foreign debt now, much less this obligation. We'll have to learn Greek!

Medicare is a little easier to adjust. Eliminate the fraud and subtract the "Family Doctor" costs, leaving what amounts to Federally provided medical benefits, paid-for by the retiree instead of an employer medical coverage.

This is basically there now, full of loopholes and outright fraud, but fixable. These lifelines are not taxable as income when you retire, because you will have already paid into them **all** your working career.

Medicaid is a necessary benefit for those who **truly need it**, and that's the key. Recent federal and State guidelines seem to have been loosened to allow more and more questionable beneficiaries. That largess needs immediate scrutiny and tightening, This would probably diminish Democrat voter roles somewhat **(I didn't really mean that, did I?)**.

The same wage-earner contribution guidelines for Social Security and Medicare deductions must apply to Family Doctor Care. In effect you are paying for your entitlement lifelines as you earn. In fact, every dollar you might earn by working or get from compo, welfare or Medicaid is treated as taxable income.

State & Federal subsidies, Grants, Welfare, Workman's Comp and Medicaid are not handouts, but along with your earned salary added, are all called **taxable income**.

The VA system can be absorbed into this scheme, with extended Veteran treatment provided through an individual annual "Vet Military Grant" to provide insured medical care beyond the Family Doctor level.   .

DEFINED & CONTROLLED IMMIGRATION

The 1965 Hart-Cuellar Immigration act, a Congressional bi-partisan bill signed by Lyndon B. Johnson, may be suitable for this century too with some exceptions added today. Most notably, it must be controlled, not a funnel for anyone who can climb the southern fence or those unfortunates, called refugees. That's not controlled in any sense now.

Prior to the 1965 revision, US legal immigration quotas were 10% annually with immigration from some countries restricted entirely. This act allowed immigration from every corner of the earth. That would be OK, but this administration keeps increasing the annual quotas. They were increased to 30% and by the 2010 census to almost 40%. That of course doesn't include those who sneak in. Why?

Could it be that they are trying to stuff Democratic voter rolls? It is estimated that by 2042, the traditional American population will no longer be the majority, but a homogeneous mixture of many nationalities who want to create their **home away from back home** right here, rather than become new American Americans.

Traditional America is vanishing by the constant Progressive pressure to increase Democrat voter rolls, encouraging an uncontrolled "welcome aboard our sinking ship" approach.

"All you have to do is vote how, when and where we tell you and you'll get a lot of free shit". This country did alright before, without the uncontrolled jailbreak from reality to nirvana.

Alien Invasion

It seems that there are only a few countries left that have preserved their heritage and tradition, and they seem to stay out of the limelight — away from conflict.

They also seem to not give a damn much about what's going on in the rest of the world. There doesn't seem to be a large influx of other cultures trying to take them over, or maybe the invaders have willingly been assimilated into the host's way of doing things.

The US has millions of illegals trying to meld into the background here. They want to stay out of sight and be a neighborhood from back home, wherever that was.

They don't want to be Americans. They want to be Egyptian-Americans, Ethiopian-Americans, Chinese-Americans, Cuban-Americans and African-Americans. We tend to take care of them because our government is a nanny state.

There are large populations of Koreans and Russians. many Chinese, Vietnamese, Indian and Middle Eastern expatriates and refugees from everywhere.

Not listed above are the majority of the early European settlers here who have joined cultures with one language, and assimilated their ideas into what we call America.

These people are joined together by a desire to be one nation. Different parts of town harbor ethnic roots, but everybody speaks English in school, on the street and in business. They don't try to change America. They want to be part of it.

There's parts of today's Philadelphia where the street signs are in Korean. There are parts of Miami where no one speaks American. Their Facebook drivel is in Spanish, not American. City schools have classes taught in Spanish for the Cuban, Haitian and Mexican kids.

Recognizing Ebonics caused the Oakland, California School Board to give up that notion years ago, due to a nationwide outcry against Black English being taught. Oakland clarified their position, but it clearly fired up those who don't want a multicultural America, but a nation where many cultures **must** assimilate into the one that's already here, the most sought after outpost on our planet.

Somehow that concept has waned in the latter quarter of the 20th Century until today, going from one end of a major city to the other is like going from one country to another, from Cape Town to Reykjavik.

A puzzling aspect of this diversity is the way the Chinese have managed to have a "Chinatown" in every major city in the world. Their home away from their homeland is accepted willingly, for several reasons, I think.

They are always there, but never demanding. They are always self sufficient, usually good neighbors and industrious businesspeople. They don't force their culture on others and yet they have assimilated worldwide with little controversy?

I don't believe we've ever made any concessions to their ethnicity or a special education curriculum to help them. They always seem to be good citizens and all their kids graduate and speak American English, **clearly**.

Illegal aliens of every stripe have wheedled themselves into American society and consciousness today, to the point where we are supporting them now and the damned government is trying to give them amnesty, so we can keep supporting their illegal needs legally. I have nothing against any of them personally, only in how they have learned how to work our increasingly Socialist country to the point that they are taxing our overextended resources, patience and resolve.

Past US Presidents had the courage to send them back. In the 1930s Herbert Hoover repatriated over a million Mexicans even though 60% of them were US Citizens.

I'm not advocating that, because the Mexican is usually a good citizen and they are hard workers. In 1954 President Eisenhower instituted what was called "Operation Wetback" where illegal Mexicans were sent back in trains and boats way down into Mexico and all done with less than two thousand Border Patrol agents. A million went back, 650,000 voluntarily.

I bet if you look into your kids "Politically Correct" history books, these pieces of our history are not widely discussed, if at all.[27]

Politicians in 1965 eliminated the annual 100,000 quota of legal immigrants into the US. I believe at that time, they had to have a sponsor here and had to have a job lined up and also had to learn English and some of our history before becoming a Naturalized American citizen.

Most of them were from Eastern European countries. Not Today. We seem to soak up the refugees from every conflict worldwide and not count them in the list as immigrants. Most of them should be sent back if they don't assimilate by the time their back-hometown has calmed down.

Europe is already overrun with people who want to undo European culture and redo it as a new outpost of the Middle East. Ask them how their traditional culture has been overrun by newcomer intransigence to assimilate. Paris just had another reminder that they should've locked their immigration doors long ago. Are we being conned into following their misguided do-gooder efforts?

We had that here back in 1980, when Fidel Castro emptied his prisons and allowed thousands of dissatisfied Cubans to scramble across the straits between Havana and South Florida.

The Mariel Boatlift brought many new criminals along with the legitimate refugees to help continue the exploding 70's and 80's drug wars in South Florida.

We don't need to repeat that now with undercover ISIS getting a free ride from Obama. He's already taxing our resources with the South American influx across the southwest borders. How many bad guys are in that bunch? It's got to stop!

Entering this country through New York harbor and Ellis Island was one our heralded and cherished traditions. Why did that change?

Wikkipedia states that it was political maneuvering back in the Roosevelt era to allow the uncontrolled influx with the promise of citizenship in order to generate votes. Why do you think the Presidency was reduced to two terms after he passed on? Gee! Do you think this is happening today?

Cost For New Voters[28]

$11 to $22 billion is spent on welfare to support illegal aliens each year.

Illegal households only pay about one-third the amount of federal taxes that legal households pay.

Illegal households create a net fiscal deficit at the federal level of more than $10 billion a year. If given amnesty, this number could grow to more than $29 billion.

$1.9 billion dollars a year is spent on food-assistance programs such as food stamps and free school lunches for illegal aliens.

$1.6 billion is spent on the federal prison and court system for illegal aliens. Currently the Obama administration is letting the semi-good guys out!

$2.5 billion dollars a year is spent on Medicaid for illegal aliens.

About 21 percent of the population of U.S. prisons is classified as "noncitizens" from Mexico, Colombia, Cuba and the Dominican Republic."

A possible solution might be to immediately cease all welfare programs for illegals, but give them 5-year temporary Green work cards and a place in line at Ellis Island, where they must pass the required steps to becoming a citizen, including paying payroll taxes and into the normal entitlements — in English.

Eliminate sanctuary cities and require employers to hire only Green-Card carrying immigrant employees. **Prohibit further immigration until all these people are either naturalized or repatriated.**

Any illegal alien must wait twice as long to become a US citizen as those who've obeyed our rules. Once they become taxpaying citizens of their new resident state, then legal residency can be established.

Since our immigration system has been so mismanaged and out of balance, I feel that now is the time to close it altogether until the current crop of New Americans is assimilated.

The term Refugee has been misused and should be eliminated as a qualification until we can determine why somebody is shooting at them — maybe it should be us?

Refugees can be **interned** here for their safety. If they can be vetted for residency, then and only then, they can stand in the new immigrant line, but with added observation.

In today's world, any incoming foreigner needs a much more thorough screening by embassies as they wait for a US Visa. We should now require a visa for **any and all travel to the US**.

Thus, all Muslim migrants and refugees, **unless thoroughly vetted**, must go elsewhere until this eternal Jihad is finally over. It has been going on for at least the last 1,500 years now, but I feel the end is near — maybe by 3016.

INVIOLATE TRADITIONS

Since creation, as mankind began to reason for himself and to fend for himself — alone at first, then in tribes, kingdoms, nations and on and on until today, this **American Mankind** of ours is surviving, but in a less than satisfactory manner with outcomes OK for some, but not everyone — **conflict prevails**!

The Big Bang theory and Creationism all refer to the same thing — the origins of mankind and its progress on this planet. They are one and the same thing, but from different viewpoints.

Consider for instance, the fact that the teachings espoused by organized religion are all just parables prepared by ancient teachers to instruct followers — the students of the time.

They are interpretations of their own particular history and experience. They were **stories** told to others to induce them to follow the teachers' paths to a **perceived wellbeing.** Parables are **stories** created to teach **their "right way"** by analogy. The teacher was an Apostle, a Mullah, Rabbi or a Priest — maybe a carpenter.

Keep in mind the viewpoint of these teachers. They were the **"learned men"** of their time, whose oratory attracted followers, who in turn began to live by their mentor's teachings. **The time is the antiquity of mankind, all articulated <u>by parables of THAT time.</u>**

There was precious little science then, other than learning how to start a fire or grow a bean maybe. As centuries passed, science began to creep into man's evolution — hence the precision of ancient undertakings, like the mathematics used in designing and building pyramids.[29]

As man's intellect evolved, so did his quest for discovery. He began to look into the "how or why" of things. This was the beginning of independent inquiry leading to theoretical discovery — the "Big Bang Theory" and all of today's scientific knowledge.

In the abstract, mankind followed ancient parables to guide everyday interactions and they also followed scientific precepts as they evolved, when delving into "How does that work?"

Today's arguments neglect to include man's capacity to think in abstract terms and the absolutes of science **within the same mind.**

Fundamentalist teachings should always be tempered with the thought that they were probably not meant to be anymore than generalizations — not the contemporary Muslim Sharia absolutes of ISIS, Hamas, Al-Qaida, Boko Haram or any other modern Fundamental crusade.

Did Moses part the Red Sea — 3266 years ago?

That parable (story) is used in **fundamental** teaching to describe, in apocryphal terms, the march of the Jews to safety, driven by the Egyptian Pharaoh, waaaaaaay back around 1250 BC!

There was no science intended in that story. There probably was a drought and Moses got lucky. In the abstract, Moses was God's messenger back then in 1250 BCE. (Oops!)

The key to understanding the Religious mess our world is in today, is in realizing that demigods are using ingrained Fundamental (= ancient) teaching as a tool to further conflict and to pressure those who don't think for themselves, into believing their religion wants them to take over everyone else's religion and that their religion is the only way.

When I attended Catholic grammar school (1940 to 1948), the good Nuns taught that you weren't going to heaven if you were a Protestant???

The basic need for organized religion, any religion or all religion for that matter, is to teach developing minds how to interact with others in a civilized and moral manner, in today's world. It really doesn't matter how you learned to **"Do unto others as you would have them do unto you,"** as long as you learn it — and live by it.

You don't need an organized religion to learn and to follow that precept. Regularly attending one though, might keep you focused on the concept.

No, one, organized religion or belief is better than another. Their only purpose is to engrain that one simple and basic concept into developing minds. Those Bishops, Mullahs, Rabbis or organized religious leaders by any other name, that perpetuate their beliefs through use of the sword (or today's car-bomb), are deluded by their lack of contemporary thought. They don't seem to be able to think beyond ancient Fundamental parables.

Tradition

"An inherited pattern of thought or action"
"A specific practice of long standing."

It is a historical fact that this nation was founded with the notion that we are **"One nation under God"**, and yet we bow to those who are offended by that thought. Too bad — get over it or move!

Fortunately we are not forced, at least not yet, in our semi-civilized world, to believe one way or another. What is objected to in America is a perceived lack of separation of Church affairs from State affairs which has pushed the atheists and ACLU to litigate the issue.

If tradition has been established by the annual display of a Christmas tree on the Courthouse lawn, that display is criticized by some who have no tradition of their own, and therefore say they are offended.

Political Correctness steps in and tries to soothe the nay-sayers feelings by forbidding open displays of religious beliefs in government, thereby destroying a long standing tradition, embraced by 99.9% of Americans.

The atheist could start a tradition that might endure if enough constituents agree and it's done in the proper way. Americans with African heritage have endured over the years and now Kwanza is an observed and respected annual tradition. Not originally native to this land, they are now well entrenched, have equal opportunity and have a powerful voice in their evolution **as Americans**.

Irishmen and Germans weren't native here either. Only the native Indians were. A black man is now our President. He's not our most effective leader by a long shot, but proves the worth of a people following the traditions of America.

The red people, American Indians, were screwed by new American settlers, encroaching on their land and traditions, each faction pushing them around and treating them much worse than the black man was ever treated here.

Today's America is allowing and even **encouraging ethnic separation** back into tribal states in the name of Socialist diversity. The Indian Nations stick together in their

Government Provided tribal enclaves while every city has its "Chinatown", every city has its largely black ghettos. Detroit has a burgeoning long-standing Muslim community.

While every American Tribe has its traditions, those tribes, the people of America, must come together as **one, united and strong tribe, <u>all on the same path</u>** — whatever that path turns out to be — but together!

Current, ancient, Middle Eastern conflicts are all the result of keeping **<u>tribal differences the centerpiece of their existence.</u>** That daily display of their version of "Nation Building" should be a mirror into what's starting to happen worldwide as Muslim immigrants and refugees show up everywhere.

If we allow that to continue, to be jammed down our throats as "Politically Correct Diversity", the future of America is well represented by the degraded way-of-life shared by the Sunni, Shia and Kurd tribal differences that have been festering for thousands of years. We've been going down that same path for less than 600.

Allowing the Progressive governing currently in control here to continue, further separates the ethnic identities into tribal conflict, just like the Middle East Nations have endured through all of recorded history. None of them have assimilated. Iraq is an outstanding example. No Sharia can come here.

The three factions of that country are all of the general Muslim category, but still separated for centuries, into those three main warring tribes. The Sunni version of the Muslim faith is the largest religious faction in the whole world. Today, ISIS, a strict fundamentalist version of Sunni Islam, is trying to kill them all — and us too!

Teaching children the beliefs of the "Old Tribal Ways" should be relegated, in our case, to "American History" classes in school, along with thorough studies of the Constitution and Bill of Rights we all live by today — the guidance and foresight of the "Founding Fathers" who's wisdom created the credos we strive to follow in this diverse world of today. Those young students need to thoroughly understand today's history and the evolution of religions as well.

Tradition is recognition of an event, a belief or an achievement that becomes part of who we are, over time. The sum of all these traditions represent a people as much as the geography they inhabit.

Freedom of religion is one of the precepts of American heritage. Although based on Judeo-Christian principals, tolerance for all beliefs is acceptable here so long as they fit into the generalization of **"Do Unto Others As You Would Have Them Do Unto You"**, and recognize **American laws** as inviolable[30].

Maybe we need a new amendment to our Constitution! This Nation was originally founded and organized under the principals of Judeo-Christian beliefs, which can all be enumerated by the precepts of the Ten Commandments:

1. **You shall have no other Gods before me**
2. **You shall not take the name of God in vain**
3. **You shall remember the Sabbath day**
4. **You shall honor your father and your mother**
5. **You shall not kill**
6. **You shall not commit adultery**
7. **You shall not steal**
8. **You shall not bear false witness against your neighbor**

9. You shall not covet your neighbor's wife
10. You shall not covet your neighbor's goods

All summarized by the Golden Rule:

"Do unto others as you would have them do unto you."

Following these precepts eliminates the inclusion of any aberrant interpretations or additions to our Constitution and Bill of Rights — Sharia for instance.

Gun Culture
A Unique American Tradition

I believe it was President Regan's administration that cut funding to States for Mental Care, consequently leaving them way underfunded for that. Mental facilities were closed and the nuts and loons were now homeless. They all flew their cuckoo nests.

Apparently that problem has never been readdressed and today's diagnosis is to medicate rather than cure or keep 'em locked up. Most every crime against humanity is done by aberrant minds.

Our constitution guarantees citizens the right to arm and defend themselves against assault. Unfortunately it doesn't address questions raised in modern times, like "Do we license the nuts or perpetual drunkards too, even if they haven't yet blemished their sanity record?

The NRA has staunchly resisted any attempt to diminish that tradition, to their credit. But times are changing at such a rapid rate, that new thought must be given, not to how to disarm everybody, but how to strengthen the notion that a legal gun owner is of impeccable and sane character, well trained and ready to stand with the authorities against all intruders, foreign and domestic, Jahadists, gang-bangers, druggies, race hustlers etc..

Most people don't realize just how many legal gun owners there are today in the USA. In Pennsylvania alone there were 750,000 hunting licenses issued for the November 30, 2015 opening day of the traditional annual deer hunting season. How many gun owners don't hunt? How many gun owners have more than one gun? Do some mental math and multiply that number by 50 states.

This issue must be handled without histrionics, but with intelligent discourse and long range planning. Maybe we should consider some form of the Swiss approach — every citizen is armed by the Government, and has annual training as part of their national home defense.

History posits that's why   Hitler never attacked Switzerland[31] It's claimed that the Japanese never attacked the US mainland during WW II for that very same reason.

Universal Military and Civic Service as in Switzerland or Israel might serve several needs — partisan unity and to foster a more common identity. The Homeland Security Federal Army should be **replaced** by the States' militias, in which every citizen is a member. Each citizen must initially serve in his or her State's Guard for a defined fulltime term and then in the State Reserves forever.

Symbol Of Sacrifice

A war memorial in the middle of the Mojave Desert had a traditional cross to represent the sacrifice of those who died in war to protect our other traditions, yet the governing jurisdiction there hadn't the guts to honor those men by defying the ACLU and its atheist. There was no Christ on that cross ✝.

A plywood box covered it for a time, until the cross was removed altogether to appease the ACLU's leftist non-Americans. That symbol over time, has become a worldwide tradition celebrating **sacrifice**. It's time our Congress clarified that into our law, to reaffirm it and that all of our American traditions will remain inviolate — not tinkered with by the ACLU's atheist, the UN, politically correct socialists or zealots — no matter from which swamp they evolve.

The ACLU even has **tradition** — historically defending the legal rights of citizens to object under the law to other **traditions**, perceived to pervert some constitutional provision. Their tradition is well known, but not popularly accepted. I don't know how the ACLU could symbolize that, but properly done, might be accepted as a symbol of dissent, along with burning the stars and stripes.

To remove those symbols dilutes history. Lets remove all historical references to slavery in America and to the fact that America swiped the west from native Indians and Mexico.

We bought the Louisiana Purchase from Napoleon in 1803 who just traded it away from Spain, who swiped it from the Indians I think. I'm not sure — I wasn't there.

The recent Charleston massacre by a white supremacist, homegrown terrorist kid, has again inflamed racial divide over the Confederate flag symbol. Whether you like it or not, that flag too is just part of our history and should be relegated to historical remembrance.

Should we remove that history because traditional references through symbolism might offend someone? I don't think so. It's our history — good or bad, but shouldn't symbolize any part of the current Government — no more than flying the English flag, which once symbolized us, or the Mexican flag flown over Texas, New Mexico, Arizona and California. How about flying the French flag over Louisiana and the Spanish flag over Florida? They used to own those places! Spanish flags flew from the masts of Columbus' ships. Actually Eric the Red and his Norse armada first discovered this hemisphere and landed his ships around 900 I think. I've stood by the foundation of the first church he built by the Tunulliarfik Fjord, Greenland. The Norseman's flags were long since gone, but might reside in this worlds museums too — if only we could find one.

There are quite a few flags that represent our heritage. The first "American" flag on 1775 merchant ships was of a pine tree. We have flown 47 different American flags with various configurations of stars and stripes. Those are also in museums where they belong. The ONLY flag that represents this nation today, has 50 stars and 13 red and white stripes.[32]

If we can't keep ISIS out, we may someday be flying their black flag in classrooms. We might have to get the 50 stars and stripes out of the local museums and start over by pouring Arab tea into the bay in Boston.

One of the latest Politically Correct flaps is over naming sports teams after historic Native Indian tribes. Those names are traditionally used to honor the **bravery and cunning of the Indian warrior**. How can anyone object to that?

I'm reminded of the pig farmer who was sued by new neighbors, offended by farming fumes — too bad! You can't change the bathing habits of "Porky the Pig".

The new neighbors wanted to change the traditional perfume of farms to suit their elite, citified, flatlander's politically correct sensibilities. They should've stayed where they were or better yet, just **"Go to hell".**

Should we include in that amalgam, anyone "Fundamental" who might work toward changing our tradition to suit theirs? Fundamental Muslims should stay in the Middle East where Sharia law is acceptable in some places. It will never be here. Freeloading immigrants should stay where they are as well. Let their anchor babies anchor them where they were.

Why do people worldwide, die trying to reach our shores to become Americans? Is it because of our historic American traditions, our Constitution and Bill of Rights — maybe because of our newest tradition, "Free shit and a Phone?"

— **30** —

END NOTES

Please take note of the fact that these endnotes don't have any of the Official or recommended style formatting. They're not Politically nor Academically correct — and I don't care.

---

1   The X Files
2   Satire by C3 to illustrate a point.
3   The Senate attached legislation to it they knew wouldn't pass — "Political Poker," while illegal alien criminals in Sanctuary Cities hide out under local Government's protection!
4   John Sununu
5   Bill Connerly 12/25/13 in FORBES
6   http://www.theblaze.com/stories/2015/01/26/cbo-national-debt-to-hit-19-1-trillion-under-obama/
7   https://en.wikipedia.org/wiki/Service_Employees_International_Union
8   https://en.wikipedia.org/wiki/List_of_countries_by_total_length_of_pipelines
9   https://rankingamerica.wordpress.com/
10   http://www.huffingtonpost.com/wm-robert-irvin/snail-darter-politics_b_4833457.html
http://www.wsj.com/articles/SB10001424052970204731804574384731898375624
11   https://en.wikipedia.org/w/index.php?title=Government_agency&oldid=694726029
12   http://www.washingtonpost.com/politics/obama-to-propose-combining-agencies-to-shrink-federal-government/2012/01/13/gIQAHsLqvP_story.html
http://www.washingtonpost.com/blogs/federal-eye/post/trade-offices-targeted-in-reorganization-plan/2011/06/09/AGaCQ7MH_blog.html
13   Excerpts from Wikipedia —
http://www.socialstudieshelp.com/Lesson_86_Notes.htm
14   http://www.socialstudieshelp.com/Lesson_86_Notes.htm
15   http://en.wikipedia.org/wiki/Great_Wall_of_China
16   (which includes the Border Patrol and US Coast Guard)
17   Defense Advanced Research Projects Agency
18   Percentage is a guess on my part. It was so long ago, I don't remember!
19   Fox News
20   http://www.crossroad.to/text/articles/whpwans97.html
http://www.crossroad.to/Books/BraveNewSchools/3-NewThinking.htm
21   The Monroe Doctrine was a U.S. foreign policy regarding domination of the American continent in 1823. It stated that further efforts by European nations to colonize land or interfere with states in North or South America would be viewed as acts of aggression, requiring U.S. intervention.......Wikkipedia
22   https://www.globalpolicy.org/component/content/article/185/40586.html
23   A political system governed by a few people — Word Web

24   https://hookandclaw.wordpress.com/2011/09/25/prescott-bushs-treason/

25   (New Testament) the scene of the final battle at the end of the world.

26   "Keep It Simple Stupid"

27   www.csmonitor.com/2006/0706/p09s01-coop.html/(page)/1

28   Center for Immigrant Studies - 2/11/09 by Ron Livingston

29   2630 BC — 2630 BCE if you are Politically Correct — 4645 years ago! The
      Progressives even want to change that delineation of history today by saying it
      was BCE (Before Common Era) and not BC. What a joke! Sorry fellas. That
      tradition stays. It's BC!

30   "Not capable of being violated or infringed" — Word Web

31   http://world.time.com/2012/12/20/the-swiss-difference-a-gun-culture-that-
      works/

32   http://www.ushistory.org/betsy/flagfact.html